THE AMERICAN NEWNESS

CULTURE AND POLITICS
IN THE AGE OF EMERSON

THE WILLIAM E. MASSEY SR.
LECTURES IN THE HISTORY OF
AMERICAN CIVILIZATION
1985

THE
AMERICAN
NEWNESS

CULTURE AND POLITICS
IN THE AGE OF EMERSON

IRVING HOWE

HARVARD UNIVERSITY PRESS

CAMBRIDGE, MASSACHUSETTS

LONDON, ENGLAND

1986

Library of Congress Cataloging-in-Publication Data

Howe, Irving.
The American newness.

(The William E. Massey Sr. lectures in the history
of American civilization; 1986)
Includes index.
1. Emerson, Ralph Waldo, 1803–1882—Influence.
2. American literature—19th century—History and
criticism.
3. United States—Intellectual life—1789–1865.
I. Title.   II. Series.
PS1633.H6   1986   814'.3   85-24903
ISBN 0-674-02640-3 (alk. paper)

Designed by Gwen Frankfeldt

To the Memory of J. V. Cunningham
Colleague, Teacher, Friend

PREFACE

To confront American culture is to feel oneself encircled by a thin but strong presence: a mist, a cloud, a climate. I call it Emersonian, an imprecise term but one that directs us to a dominant spirit in the national experience. Hoping to engage this spirit, I am not sure anyone can even grasp it. How grasp the very air we breathe? Nor do I add a mite of scholarship to the study of nineteenth-century American culture. I want merely to understand: What were they up to, Emerson and his disciples? What drove them, what blinded them? And, pieties apart, what can they still mean to us?

My hope is to advance a somewhat novel or at least eccentric view of "the newness," as the period of the 1830s and 1840s came to be called; and to do this through a juxtaposition of narrative and analysis which does not always end in the explicit. But through the weavings of this little book there emerges, I think, an idea.

My greatest debt, recorded here with pleasure, is to Professor David Herbert Donald, the distinguished historian who, as head of the American Civilization program at Harvard University, invited me to give the Massey Lectures on which this book is based.

Several young friends—David Bromwich, Nicholas Howe, and Nicolaus Mills—have read the manuscript with friendly care and critical eye. My gratitude goes out to them.

Professors John McAleer, Robert Richardson, and Joel Porte helped me with several sources. From the work of a number of scholars—Stephen Whicher, Leo Marx, Taylor Stoehr—I learned and borrowed. Professor Frederick Amtczak, to whom a particular debt is acknowledged in the Notes, has been exceptionally generous. I thank them all.

When nature looks natural, that is
the end . . . It is the beginning
of something else.

—Pasolini, in his film *Medea*

It is impossible to extricate oneself
from the questions in which your age
is involved. You can no more keep out
of politics than you can keep out of
the frost.

—Emerson (1862)

I

EMERSON
AND
HAWTHORNE

EMERSON AND HAWTHORNE, born only a year apart, are often cast as polar opposites. So they are, but opposites subtly, deeply, linked. Their opinions, temperaments, and styles of speech are radically different; yet they emerge out of the same historic matrix, inherit roughly the same problems of faith, and respond to shared cultural difficulties. Each hovers across the other's path, not very sympathetic, yet often attentive.

New England culture was visibly coming apart by the time Emerson and Hawthorne began to write. They grew up in an atmosphere of "religious crisis," the breakdown of a once authoritative structure of belief; a time, as Emerson wrote, "when all the antique Hebraisms and customs are going to pieces." An undertow of secular thought had begun to pull both writers a little closer to, though not quite into, the world of modernity. Neither Emerson nor Hawthorne could take Puritanism as the sufficient truth it had been for their ancestors, yet they retained some jagged portions of the Puritan world view—jagged because freed from the obligations of coherence. Hawthorne knew this better than Emerson, sensing how strongly all of us, even spiritual rebels like the young Emerson, remain in the grip of the past. Which is one reason that Hawthorne seems to cast a shadow of skepticism over Emerson's luminous pages.

The religious crisis the two writers inherited, Hawthorne neither struggled against nor submitted to: he simply stayed with it, accepting its burdens as his fate. Had he heard talk about a religious crisis, he would, I suspect, have said—if he had troubled to say *anything*—that we are born to the circumstances that mold our lives and must abide them, since we have nothing else. To think of "transcending" what we would now call "our cultural situation" would surely have struck him as idle. He lived out his circumstances, acknowledging them as the mate of his spirit, sometimes with skepticism, sometimes with a spark of rebellion. The discomforts of life became the motives of art.

What Hawthorne shared with the Puritans was mostly their vexations. These made him, as Marius Bewley has nicely said, a "Puritan agnostic," radically uncertain about the possibilities of gaining knowledge or reaching truth. Living in what he took to be a weightless time, he found in Puritan New England an occasionably usable past. The life of the Puritans had weight; their thought, gravity; their morality, empirical bearing. But the imaginative use to which Hawthorne put early New England is often devious, beginning with fraternal recognitions and ending with sly dissociations. If not quite at ease with the Puritans, he was less at ease with his Concord neighbors, fine transcendental figures all but deluded into supposing that, through an exercise of spirit, they could elevate themselves to a new state of being. Neither Calvinist depravity nor Transcendental mildness could long withstand Hawthorne's corrosive skepticism. He believed, finally, in little but the bond between men and women lost to their natures. Perhaps that was enough.

It is wonderful that in a country which makes the refusal of history into a first principle, our first major writer of fiction should have grappled with his provincial history as if it held the weight of the ages. The past shapes and deforms, the past *is* the present: so Hawthorne felt. But Emerson would have no truck with the kind of feelings he describes as "retrospective." Calling himself "a seeker with no Past at his back"—a piece of impudence possible only to an American—Emerson wrote: "it is a mischievous notion that we are come late into nature, that the world was finished long ago." Hawthorne, by contrast, believed that everyone comes late into nature.

Hawthorne could see the past in its alien integrity, and this enabled him to use if for problematic ends. In *The Scarlet Letter* setting and character are sometimes at odds, as if a woman of quasi-modernist sensibility were being thrust unsuspectingly into a Calvinist milieu. Hawthorne made Puritan New England a place not of moral grandeur but of decline and disorder. Somewhat like writers of the modernist era—though he was not a modernist—he could realize his values only through images of violation. His characters are subject to the Puritan rigors but cannot reach the balm of grace, so that they must fall back upon their disturbed inner selves, always for Hawthorne an occasion for mistrust.

The Puritan community in *The Scarlet Letter* imposes on Hester Prynne a defined punishment; once this limit is achieved, the community lapses into a condition close to passivity, unable to help or harm her. Its rituals of judgment have been exhausted, but it is precisely beyond these rituals, or any other fixed modes of judgment, that Hawthorne wishes to go. In stories like "The Maypole of Merry Mount," "Young Goodman Brown," and "The Minister's Black Veil," the Puritan community serves as a field of disturbance, spotted at times with perversity. The writer obsessed with his native history becomes a virtuoso of breakdown.

Consider the brilliant fable "The Minister's Black Veil." The Reverend Mr. Hooper, minister of a New England village in the middle eighteenth century, suddenly and for no declared reason puts a piece of black crepe over his face and, for the rest of his life, refuses to take it off. This gesture proclaims the minister's sinfulness, though we are allowed no clear understanding of what that sin might be, unless, as we come to suspect, it be a savoring of sin. Nor does Mr. Hooper take any of the accredited recourses of faith: he does not confess, he engages in no penance. Avoiding the conventions of his faith, he tries to establish a convention of his own, which in the

Puritan setting must appear as melodrama. His black veil proclaims him to be a great sinner, or one more conversant with sin than are his fellow townsmen, all mere sinful creatures without veils. But how does Mr. Hooper presume to know? How does any mortal?

The veiled minister sends a throb of excitement, perhaps an erotic thrill, through his congregation. "Dying sinners cried aloud for Mr. Hooper, and would not yield their breath until he appeared; though ever, as he stooped to whisper consolation, they shuddered at the veiled face so near their own." Hawthorne is quietly savage in showing how the minister's false penance betrays him into ever greater eloquence, itself a sign of bad faith. Now "a man apart from men," Mr. Hooper seems intent upon *distinguishing* himself in sin, quite as some of Emerson's friends wished to distinguish themselves in spotlessness. Contrition becomes display.

I read this story as a signal of crack-up, the subtle violation of Puritan norms by a Puritan agent. But the story's power also derives from a canny anticipation of a peculiarly modern style of display: the vanity of literary people declaring "the tragic view of life" as if their black veils were certificates of depth, or the vanity of celebrities enhancing their fame through conspicuous confessions of misdeeds.

In "The Minister's Black Veil" Hawthorne exhibits two distinct, but related, varieties of moral disturbance: one depicting a Puritanism that has begun to undo itself, the other anticipating a time when there is little left to undo. Meanwhile, fixed in his troubled present, he keeps a nice distance from both the recreated past and the glimpsed future, with a trained shrewdness that, extended sufficiently, can become a mode of comprehension. Which may be an instance of the gains a writer can extract from cultural losses he must endure.

Emerson, taking a sharply different course, also gains much from his cultural losses.

Where Hawthorne stood still in confronting his religious crisis and, by standing still, almost made it cease to be a crisis at all, Emerson chose to shake off, or step away from, his received terms of belief. The Puritans, he felt, were "men whom God had honored with great usefulness," but their day was done; he could speak of them with warmth because he had freed himself from their grip. Now he would be on his own, to "work a pitch above his last height." He would create himself afresh, pressing the rim of consciousness, "glad to the brink of fear." A century later Scott Fitzgerald said of Jay Gatsby that he had sprung "from his Platonic conception of himself"—a remark that would have enchanted Emerson.

The differences between Hawthorne and Emerson are of judgment, opinion, impulse, speech; but not of predicament. Both struggle with a spiritual isolation that is in part a legacy of Calvinism, in part the consequence of living in a society that has yet to form sufficient tributaries of social connection. Hawthorne's best short fictions deal with the costs of the isolated self; nothing in Emerson's journals is more poignant than his repeated self-excoriation for failing to show sufficient warmth to friends. The burden of isolation is of course a central theme in American literature: Hawthorne copes with it through the closing of small human circles; Emerson, through invocations of selfhood grounded in a spiritualized nature. What links these seemingly distant writers, transcending their clashes of opinion, is a devotion to *inwardness,* a risky, powerful mode of personal existence that, in its nineteenth-century romantic forms, is just starting to undergo historical test.

Emerson took fragments of his religious experience— Puritan fervor, Unitarian rectitude—and fused them into an intimation of a sublimity at once private and cosmic, passing beyond Christianity and grazing secular intelligences. The Emerson of the 1830s was unwilling to settle for anything like Hawthorne's grim truce with circumstance. He propelled himself onto a journey free of mere destination, a perpetual motion of spirit. Often enough this was more desire than achievement, but sometimes everything came together for him, as in the dazzling essay, "Circles."

Repudiating "historical Christianity," Emerson dismissed the image of "our God of tradition . . . our God of rhetoric." Did he thereby quite abandon Christianity? In a historicist move that was hardly in keeping with his usual depreciation of history, Emerson proposed to incorporate the moral conquests of Christianity within a new spirituality even as it ruthlessly shed theological doctrine. In this purified faith a young seeker might find that "Within and Above are synonymous," a notion that forms a central religious affirmation of the nineteenth century. So a modest difference could be established between abandoning Christianity and foreseeing its supercession. The old gods become emeriti, a retirement also favored by Emerson's literary offspring—as in Whitman's amused proposal that we take those gods "for what they are worth and not a cent more" and Stevens' secular anthropology in "Sunday Morning."

Emerson stakes everything on intuitions of divinity— unsympathetic critics might say, on mere sentiments of faith. His great heresy appears in an 1832 journal entry:

> You must be humble because Christ says, "Be humble." "But why must I obey Christ?" . . . "Because your own heart teaches the same thing he taught." "Why then shall I not go to my own heart?"

That last sentence, with its ring of triumph, apparently struck Emerson as decisive; but it can be countered, and one way is to suggest that if Christ had not first spoken "the same thing," Emerson's heart might not have known to intuit His teaching. But for Emerson, primal intuitions seem to have no history.

The audacious sentences I have just quoted constitute a wager on authenticity as the source of truth, or on the superiority of authenticity even to truth, if—as Emerson seems to acknowledge as a possibility—authenticity and truth come into opposition. Be faithful to the depths, and your heart will speak with the melodies of goodness. Where Emerson's ancestors ascribed infallibility to scripture, he ascribed it to the inner voice. But how, asks one critic, can "random moments of insight transfer man as a temporal being into a semblance or replica of God while [man] still exists in a world of time and space?" How Emerson would have answered, or whether he would have troubled to, I am not sure; perhaps by suggesting mildly that when you are quite true to yourself, your nature, and your being, then your moments of insight are no longer "random" but decisive.

It may be that we have reached a point here where the secular and religious minds cannot engage with each other. To a secular mind it seems inevitable that there be a frequent tension, or disjunction, between truth and authenticity and, indeed, that a serious inner life entails an effort to bring the two, if not into complete harmony, then at least into a vital relation. To the religious mind, I suppose, the tension between truth and authenticity is also to be acknowledged as a fact of experience, but there remains the beckoning possibility of a subjective life that meets the demands of revelation, so that someone like Emerson could suppose his trust in inwardness was a way of realizing Christ's own standards.

Emerson recognized that some critics thought he wanted "a rejection of all standards, and mere antinomianism." His reply to this was that "the law of consciousness abides," a remark that may be glossed by another: "They call it Christianity, I

call it consciousness." There is, it seems, a continuity of the
moral sense, and this continuity can be seen as having its own
"history," apart from faith or system. Elsewhere Emerson says
that a friend challenged his trust in impulse by asking what "if
these impulses" are "from below, not from above." Emerson's
answer still bears a lively touch of scandal:

> "They do not seem to me to be such; but if I am the Devil's
> child, I will live then from the Devil." No law can be sacred to
> me but that of my nature.

Again, the stage of Concord is darkened by a neighboring
shadow, Hawthorne in the guise of Young Goodman Brown
who also decides to "live from the Devil" because he has con-
cluded, on slender evidence, that he and just about everyone
else are the Devil's children. To which Emerson might retort
that if one is truly attuned to the inner voice, it will annul
traditional dualisms, such as that between God and the Devil,
and give the moral law a more secure foundation than mere
compliance with external authority. And the counterrebuttal?
That an external source may be supposed to transmit the accumulated experience and wisdom of the race, for we do not
always begin from the beginning; while an inner voice, mixing
memory and desire, must always begin anew, unprotected in
its innocence. In truth, however, Emerson seldom cared to
argue, he was content to reveal; so that for those of us who are
cool to revelation there remains a serious difficulty in his treat-
ment of the relation between authenticity and truth.

New England in the early nineteenth century had become a
battleground for that strife between Christian orthodoxy and
the various enthusiasms and enlightenments which were tear-
ing apart the churches of Europe. Emerson's early essays have
tonal, sometimes doctrinal points of kinship with David

Straus's effort to free Jesus from legend, Ludwig Feuerbach's shift from theology to anthropology, George Eliot's replacement of a transcendent deity by a "religion of humanity" domesticating the sacred. In these European writings, much is sacrificed in a last stand to save the core of religious life. God is relocated; Heaven is everywhere, or perhaps nowhere; belief is relieved of doctrine. Yet these writers, quite against their wishes, hasten the decline of the faith, for none can provide the comforts of totality which traditional religion could. One important difference between them and Emerson is that they tried to salvage religion through interpretation, while Emerson, who cared little or nothing about interpreting religion, was concerned with maintaining an immediate apprehension of the divine. He was also a keener tactician, skipping past the irritations of argument, or what some would regard as the shoals of rationalism, to achieve, in one charmed glide of intuition, an effect like unity. All experience could now be transfigured as consciousness; all consciousness lifted free from the alloys of circumstance; after which would come a bliss of spiritual exchange. "There is never a beginning, there is never an end," wrote Emerson, "to the inexplicable continuity of the web of God, but always circular power returning into itself." From which could also follow a beatitude of democracy: "the simplest person who in his integrity worships God, becomes God." An end to institutions and churches; no more sacred texts or "ambassadors to God"—only the solitary self in its sublime moments melting into the Sublime Other, that "God without medium" who may be no more than a potential of the solitary self.

But we must add to this account Emerson's troubled self-criticism: "A believer in Unity, a seer of Unity, I yet behold two." And the splendid sentence in "Circles": "I am God in nature; I am a weed by the wall." These remarks suggest that Emerson's encounters with sublimity occurred in flashes, rare and unpredictable. Waiting, patiently or not, for those moments, he also shows a tough-minded awareness of the sheer drag and waste of daily life, the wearing down of hope by time. "We must wear old shoes and have aunts and cousins." We must put up with bores who visit Concord. We must abide Thoreau's prickliness and Hawthorne's silence. We must yield a little to the ordinary.

The optative mood of Emerson's early essays can prey on the nerves. Phrases of resistance come insistently to mind: the ruthlessness of joy, the weariness of exaltation. I do not want to be harried into sublimity; let it come, if it comes. And I wish that, in the Emersonian landscape, there were rather more old shoes and aunts and cousins.

Total these discounts as you will, Emerson's regathering of the fragments of his faith still constitutes a notable intellectual maneuver. He collapsed the distinction between religious and secular, so that the exaltations of the one might be summoned for the needs of the other. He prescribed and sometimes portrayed a vibrant state of being for which neither religious nor secular is an adequate term of description. He succeeded in escaping doctrines of the sacred without having to suffer the penalties of desacrilization. For a brief moment he recreated the sense of unity that had been lost with the collapse of Puritan New England.

Emerson's faith, more luminous than substantial, stems from an inwardness that is self-subsistent and, unless willfully repressed, need never run dry. A wavering line of continuity links him with theological writers of our time: Martin Buber, eager to spark a universe of animation; Paul Tillich, in awe before "the fundament of being." Everything grows more slippery and insubstantial, and one need not be a believer to see a certain cogency in Karl Barth's remark that while modern religion may tilt toward subjectivity, the question is whether it will yield anything but an indulgence of subjectivity, what he deplores as an "undercover apotheosis of man."

The Emerson who writes as an iconoclast of "historical Christianity" is a figure of some interest, but I doubt that a scrutiny confined to his inner spiritual development—as the best recent studies of his work have been—can succeed in demonstrating his centrality for our culture. Such a scrutiny may not even beat back the many attacks, some of them serious, that have been launched against Emerson's work and reputation.

There have been brave ventures in defense, efforts to reinterpret, through gentle applications of nuance, such Emersonian notions as "correspondence" and "compensation," as well as his views regarding evil. One defense is biographical, as when Joel Porte cites a passage from Emerson's essay, "Love":

> Alas! I know not why, but infinite compunctions embitter in mature life the remembrances of budding joy . . . Every thing is beautiful seen from the point of the intellect . . . But all is sour, if seen as experience . . . In the actual world—the painful kingdom of time and place—dwell care, and canker, and fear.

To read such passages is to be reminded that Emerson had his share of pain, grief, and emptiness—perhaps more indeed than Hawthorne. Another defense comes from Newton Arvin, who shows that Emerson recognized the reality of evil quite as much as anyone needs to. Arvin finds in Emerson a capacity for moving "beyond" the dominion of evil, "beyond" the perception of tragedy, and thereby—along the lines of Plotinus and Augustine and the Bhagavad-Gita—to reach an ultimate serenity, a sheer gratitude for being. And Arvin quotes, pertinently, from Kierkegaard: "It requires moral courage to grieve; it requires religious courage to rejoice."

I sympathize with such efforts to reveal the scope of Emerson's consciousness and to dispel the notion that he denied the presence of pain and evil in human experience. And yet, even if we join in such defenses, it is hard to suppose that anyone could now take Emerson as a sufficient moral or philosophical guide—and impossible to suppose that anyone could find him very helpful in understanding the span of Western history between the time of his death and the present. Who, by now, can acquiesce in Emerson's claim that "the laws of moral nature answer to those of matter as face to face in a glass?" Who that has recently looked in a glass? Emerson's notion of "compensation" has been defended by Harold Bloom, who cites a sentence from the older Emerson saying that it means "nothing is got for nothing." Yes; but more characteristic is this remark of the early Emerson: "There is always some levelling circumstance that puts down the overbearing, the strong, the rich, the fortunate, substantially on the same ground with others." Perhaps death does that; but short of death what could Emerson have meant? As one who has spent a good part of his life looking for the "levelling circumstance" of which Emerson speaks, I can only report that thus far it has steadily eluded me.

Strong testimony against this side of Emerson comes, again, from Hawthorne, who writes of a character in *The House of Seven Gables*:

> After such wrong as [Clifford] had suffered, *there is no reparation* . . . No great mistake, whether acted or endured, in our mortal sphere, is ever really set right.

So too, apparently, thought Lydian, Emerson's wife, who, turning on his very language, wrote after the death of their son: "Dear husband, I wish I had never been born. I do not see how God can compensate me for the sorrow of existence." Did Emerson reply by sending Lydian to Plotinus? The question may seem flippant. Yet, as between Lydian and Plotinus, the heart must side with Lydian: "I do not see how God can compensate."

To rescue Emerson from his excesses and contradictions, to mark out the places where his work remains vital, we must turn to his actual situation as the first American man of letters. Emerson surrounded himself with intellectuals—free-lance writers, stray and erratic thinkers, heterodox ministers—who created a fragile avant-garde, probably the first this country has ever had. And for all his philosophical and posttheological speculation, he was acutely responsive to the social possibilities and political moods of his moment. Only by reconstituting his situation can the full magnitude of his effort be measured.

At about the time he resigned his ministry, Emerson undertook a project of astonishing boldness, one that would have enormous consequences for our culture. That this project was doomed to fail, it takes no great wisdom to recognize. Perhaps all great intellectual projects are doomed to fail. What I want to stress, from my non-Emersonian angle of vision, is that it *was* great, a new and heroic "errand into the wilderness." Before such failure, mere success hardly signifies.

By about 1830 reflective citizens could tell themselves that, despite all the pressures of adversity and skepticism, the American republic had been secured. This was no small achievement nor, during the previous few decades, something to be taken for granted. The Founding Fathers had shared a deep anxiety, perhaps even a skepticism about the capacity of republican government to survive. And why, as pioneers of republicanism, should they not? There had been bad moments since the Revolution—first during the making of the Constitution, then during John Adams' presidency, and later, the War of

1812. Yet by the fourth decade of the century it must have seemed clear that, whatever might be wrong with American society (and much evidently was) *the republic as a historical innovation* would survive. Soon the Founding Fathers would be enshrined in myth; two of the greatest, Jefferson and Adams, had died only a few years before. For Emerson, his 1825 visit to the octogenarian Adams must have fixed itself in his imagination, confirming a common respect for our native virtues. The image that informs much of Emerson's writing in the 1830s is that of an early America, still the infant republic of independent farmers and craftsmen, still largely egalitarian in tone and, to a lesser degree, social content, still vibrating to the memory of the revolution. Half a century later Henry Adams would write:

> Except for Negro slavery, [early-nineteenth-century America] was sound and healthy in every part. Stripped for the hardest work, every muscle firm and elastic, every ounce of brain ready for use, and not a trace of superfluous flesh on his nervous and supple body, the American stood in the world as a new order.

Adams' opening phrase, "except for Negro slavery," must seem astonishing today, when we regard slavery not as an incidental blemish but as a cancerous growth. The rest of Adams' passage might be read as an idealization of the sort Americans like to grant themselves, and is therefore vulnerable to the attack launched by recent younger historians who stress that even in the Jacksonian years social inequality and class tensions grew. Still, myth is itself a reality, and American myth an American reality, the most powerful and enduring that we have. With whatever twist of irony, we can take Adams' picture of pre–Civil War America as reflecting part of the truth.

Transport yourself to the past; imagine yourself in the America of one hundred and fifty years ago; suppose yourself alive at a moment when the new nation has started feeling its strength and boasting about its virtues—a moment also when the entire Western world is in ferment, with reform bills passed, slavery under attack, kings tottering, and new theories and inventions announced. This is the time in the United States of "the newness," when people start to feel socially invigorated and come to think they can act to determine their fate. What is it like to live at such a time? The opposite of what it is like to live today.

Here in the young republic—"conceived in perfection," Richard Hofstadter wittily says, "and dedicated to progress"—a new mode of government has proved reasonably successful. It balances limited allotments of power against subterranean yearnings for utopia. The idea takes hold of a national culture, surpassing all in sight or memory. And the feeling that the United States "has come through" rests not only on self-scrutiny and pride but on the comforting comparisons that supporters as well as opponents of the French Revolution can make between the sharply different outcomes of the two revolutions. In America there is no Jacobin dictatorship, no reign of terror, no Bonapartist usurpation, no monarchical restoration. To Thomas Jefferson this is a strong argument in behalf of a moderate republicanism. In 1813 he explains to John Adams why the European

> insurrection . . . of science, talents and courage against rank and birth . . . had failed in its first effort . . . [It is] because the mob of the cities, the instrument used for [the insurrection's] accomplishment, debased by ignorance, poverty and vice, could not be restrained to rational action.

Eleven years later, writing again to Adams, Jefferson strikes a similar note:

> Our revolution commenced on more favorable ground [than those of the Europeans]. We had no occasion to search into musty records, to hunt up royal parchments, or to investigate the laws and institutions of a semi-barbarous ancestry.

After which—quite as if clearing a path for Emerson—he adds: "We appealed to [the sentiments] of nature, and found them engraved in our hearts."

This Jefferson is at once a quasi-Girondist, a defender of natural rights, and an early spokesman for what we now call "American exceptionalism." He explains that the American Revolution could succeed because it had only to concern itself with the politics of freedom or, better yet, the free operation of politics, while the French had to face the disabling social problem of a vast, impoverished lower class.

A good many years later, it is worth noting, Emerson makes precisely the same argument. Americans

> stand on the ground of simple morality, and not on the class feeling which narrows the perception of [the Europeans] . . . We are affirmative; they live under obstructions and negations. England's six points of Chartism are still postponed. They have all been granted here to begin with . . . We, in the midst of a great Revolution . . . [worked our way] through this tremendous ordeal, which elsewhere went by beheadings and massacres and reigns of terror—and [we passed] through all this . . . like a sleep, drinking our tea the while.

Together with this mode of analysis went an all but universal sentiment that America meant blessedness in a new home. Thomas Paine: "a birthday of a new world." Jefferson: "a heavenly country." And later, Whitman's lovely line: "My eyes settle the land." A complex of feelings that finds its classic expression in Jefferson's remark: "this chapter in the history of man is new." Some thirty years later would come the time of "the newness," that is, a renewal of the new.

The line of continuity between Jefferson and Emerson is not entirely clear. Amiable references to the Founding Fathers can be found in Emerson's journals, but no sign that they pressed very keenly on his imagination. Perhaps they had done their work so well that he could by now take them for granted. By

1830 Emerson finds that Jefferson "and his great mates look little already." Eleven years later:

> What business have Washington or Jefferson in this age? You must be a very dull or a very false man if you have not a better *and more advanced* policy to offer than they had. They lived in the greenness and timidity of the political experiment . . . They shocked their contemporaries with their daring wisdom: have you not something which would have shocked *them*? If not, be silent, for others have.

Far from belittling the Founding Fathers, Emerson invokes yesterday's heroes in order to brace candidates for tomorrow's heroism. He also prods himself a little as he undertakes what I call his great project. Like other Americans, he feels himself to be in the happy condition of being able to take for granted the worth and stability of the new nation—and taking it for granted, he can overreach the founders.

This must have been an extremely heady feeling, part of the national expansiveness marking the 1830s and 1840s, a time when the country found itself enlivened by a bristling crew of reformers, crusaders, utopians, and cranks. The mood of expansiveness can itself be seen as a sign that the young nation was settling into the pleasures of security.

What distinguishes Emerson from the hordes of reformers, crusaders, utopians, and cranks, making him perhaps less effective in the immediate moment but ultimately far more significant, is that he improvises a strategy for engaging the consciousness of the nation as a whole. He both responds and transforms, mirrors and exalts. He starts from where people actually are—slipping away from but still held by religious faith—and helps them move to where, roughly, they want to go: an enlightened commonality of vision justifying pride in the republic, a vision akin to, yet distinct from, religious faith. The remains of religious sentiment—ideality, yearning, spiritual earnestness—thereby become the grounding for a high public culture. And even more, for an effort to *recreate* the still-uncreated American, to make new the new republic. Emerson speaks for a permanent revolution of the spirit, he who in no ordinary sense could be called a revolutionist.*

Here, now, is the young Emerson: comfortable with the republic as the stage for his unshaped affirmations; aflame with intimations of democratic sublimity; persuaded, as not many later American writers would be, that the country is *his* by birthright, law, and nature's ordering; eager to leap across the entrenchments of his fathers so as to realize those promises of the American Revolution not even its makers could quite grasp—*promises so great as hardly to be named.* Quitting the ministry, which even with Unitarian tolerance meant confinement to ritual and set speech, Emerson becomes—exactly what? A secular evangelist, a lay preacher, a lecturer peddling visions, a man of letters breathing enlightenment, a free-lance intellectual. Seize the day: you're just in the nick of time; soon enough the American openness will shrink.

Emerson knew perfectly well that American society had faults. Everyone is familiar with "Things are in the saddle / And ride mankind," but in the same "Ode" there is a far more

---

*A student who had heard an earlier version of this account asked: "Why did Emerson have to bring all his 'baggage'—theological, philosophical, etc.—in order to declare his new vision? Why didn't he just come right out with it?"

The question is wonderful and only an American would think to ask it.

The "baggage" Emerson brought with him was no baggage at all: it was Emerson, the necessity of his moment, the ground of his desire. He was not a political man offering a program of action; he was a critical moralist, who perceived that precisely the political arrangements of the young republic offered an opportunity to brush them aside or at least brush past them, in order to declare the wild thought of a new human possibility. No one ever approaches the future without "baggage," not even the Emerson who had rashly called himself "a seeker with no Past at my back."

shattering line: "Things are of the snake." The world of "commodity," he says, is the province of Satan. These attacks are harsh; worse yet was said by Emerson about the grasping America of his day. But it was a tacit—if, as time would show, also a shaky—premise of his enterprise that the flaws of his society did not seem so grave or intractable as to block that reformation of being which he saw as the imperative, the glowing possibility, of the moment. For nearly two decades Emerson wrote and spoke from this controlling persuasion. Whitman, in a great line, would give it flesh: "I find letters from God dropt in the street, and every one is sign'd by God's name." And they knew exactly what was in those letters.

In the years of the newness it was possible for otherwise sober people to believe that mankind, or at least mankind in post-revolutionary America, had disentangled itself from historical conditions—is that not the proclaimed goal of all serious revolutions? The time was at hand "to recognize man's consciousness of himself as the highest divinity." This sentence reads like the young Emerson; actually it comes from the young Marx. It hardly matters. For at long last, in the blaze of the early nineteenth century, it could seem a real, a true project to create what Emerson called "the Central Man," the new American, unalienated and self-subsistent, the first in history. "The Central Man" would be the companion of a God lodged in his soul; he would be ripe with spirit; he would reach out for knowledge and freedom, a very Bulkington of democratic buoyancy. Traditional agencies of authority, traditional manners of slavishness, traditional stigmata of caste, traditional postures of submission—all would be thrust aside, "to make way," as the historian George Fredrickson says, "for man himself in his natural perfection." That's the needed phrase: man himself in his natural perfection, an agent of fraternity stepping out from the ranks of the democratic revolution. Man would know, wrote Emerson, "that the world exists for you" and, knowing that, be ready "to build therefore your own world." ❧

Greater presumption still: there would be a new kind of revolution, sweeping past the first one of Washington and Jefferson.

> All spiritual or real power makes its own place. Revolutions of violence . . . are scrambles merely.

> The revolutions that impend over society are not now from ambition and rapacity, from impatience of one or another form of government, but from new modes of thinking, which shall recompose society after a new order, which shall animate labor by love and science, which shall destroy the value of many kinds of property, and replace all property within the dominion of reason and equity.

What Washington and Jefferson had enabled institutionally, Emerson would now bring to fruition in the sphere of the spirit, and therefore in the life of the culture.

Here is a passage from Emerson that brings us to the heart of the matter:

> After all the deduction is made for our frivolities and insanities, there still remains [in America] an organic simplicity and liberty . . . which offers opportunity to the human mind not known to any other region.

The time had come to affirm "the unsearched might of man," the revolution of and beyond all revolutions. Had there ever been such a time before?

To see Emerson in this way is to challenge the common belief that he proposed a withdrawal from public life, ignored the force of social conditions, subordinated the multiplicity of social forms and relations to a spiritualized egomania or "imperial self." Such a familiar judgment might carry weight if we were to consider Emerson an ordinary reformer or antireformer, that is, a social thinker of the familiar sort. It has much less point with regard to the Emerson of the 1830s. If we see him, in those years, as a self-elected legatee of a democratic revolution begun but not completed several decades earlier—indeed, as the critic-prophet enlarging the scope of liberation in ways that both fulfill and surpass the claims of the Founding Fathers—then the usual adverse judgments of reformers and liberals lose much of their force. We should recognize, to borrow O. W. Firkins' brilliant phrase, that as critic-prophet, Emerson's "hunger was not greedy precisely because it was insatiable." There is a line of continuity from Firkins to Stephen Whicher's remark that Emerson was "a believer in unseizable possibilities." All of which would suggest that while the possibilities Emerson saw were really there, the moment for seizing them—if indeed they could be seized—might soon slip away.

It may reinforce my argument if I provide some comparisons likely to shock or irritate Emerson's admirers. All spokesmen for movements of historical transformation claim they are not merely replacing one mode of class domination by another; they insist that their "final" end, their heart's desire, is to create a new order of mankind out of the historical process, a new order which once and for all will banish every mode of social and moral oppression. Here is Robespierre speaking to the Convention:

> We want to substitute, in our land, morality for egotism; probity for honor; principles for customs; ethics for propriety; the rule of reason for the tyranny of fashion . . . spiritual grandeur for vanity; love of glory for love of money . . . truth for brilliance.

Here, a century and a quarter later, is Trotsky:

> It is difficult to predict the extent of self-government which the man of the future may reach . . . Man will become immeasurably stronger, wiser and subtler . . . The average human type will rise

to the heights of an Aristotle, a Goethe, or a Marx. And above
this ridge new peaks will rise.

And here, in 1931, is Ben-Gurion:

> The most important contribution that [the labor Zionist]
> movement has made has been, not the new ideology we
> brought to Zionist thought . . . but, it appears to me, the
> creation of a new type of man. For this man Zionism is not
> simply a philosophy . . . but *a question of life and death* in the
> fullest implication of these terms, a problem of personal life, and
> a problem of national life.

Take for granted the differences among these political
figures, and take further for granted the differences between all
three of them and Emerson, the essayist of Concord. Yet there
remain striking parallels in rhetoric and, more problematically,
intent, as if to imply that all revolutions, simply by being
revolutions, chart related sequences of possibility: chart aspi-
rations and delusions that are built into their very natures.

Now, Emerson refused to suppose that any historical moment or condition was necessary to his undertaking, refused,
in his buoyant early period, to grant vetoes to circumstance.
Yet the pragmatic side of Emerson was very shrewd, and he
quickly spotted those aspects of American experience—the
free-floating religious energies, the consolidation of republican institutions, the glow of revolutionary promise surviving
the death of the Founding Fathers—which would give temporal urgency, a quickening spur to enactments of his vision. He
came, this benign revolutionary of consciousness, at a moment
when the country seemed ready to confront the questions that,
decades later, Henry Adams would list in his classical chapter
on "American Ideals":

> Could [America] transmute its social power into the higher
> forms of thought? Could it provide for the moral and intellec-
> tual needs of mankind? Could it take permanent political shape?

Could it give new life to religion and art? Could it create and maintain in the mass of mankind those habits of mind which had hitherto belonged to men of science alone? . . . Nothing less than this was necessary for its complete success.

Such questions are intelligible only against the backdrop of the American Revolution, and to say that in effect they are Emerson's questions is to recognize that this nonpolitical man who disliked the whole apparatus of politics was in his own way one of the most political of Americans. Prophet of "unseizable possibilities," caller for that revolution of the spirit which encompasses and dwarfs all other revolutions, he set the agenda for generations to come. It remains.

For Emerson the world was still young, still fresh and uncrowded. Forests were within walking distance of his house. Belatedness was a European malady. Spaciousness was our continent's privilege. If you had room in which to be lonely, you had room in which to become a self.

Compare this with some characteristic laments of twentieth-century writers:

José Ortega y Gasset. "The cities are full of inhabitants, the houses full of tenants . . . What previously was . . . no problem begins now to be an everyday one, to find room."

Nicola Chiaromonte. "Not finding room is an agonizing experience . . . The others are already there, they occupy all, or almost all, the available space . . . On an astoundingly humble level, we must fight to occupy the little space we need."

Paul Valéry. "The inhabitant of the great urban centers reverts to a state of savagery—that is, of isolation."

Emerson lived in a different world. The goal of fulfilling the Revolution gained vibrancy from his sense that nature (I quote from Robert Heilbroner in a different context) "is peopled with spirits and living presences . . . endowed with the capacity for suffering and rejoicing." To struggle for the self-realization or, as Emerson put it, the "self-union" of man: this was the looming promise of the Revolution, of the whole democratic enterprise.

For Emerson's experiment, Hawthorne provides a "control" of realism, shadowing hopes with doubts, enthusiasms with quizzical silence. Yet the story is more complex. A side of Hawthorne succumbs to democratic, even utopian desires; a side of Emerson bristles with country skepticism. In a vital culture antagonists can end as impersonators of one another.

In some obvious sense Emerson's project failed. It failed because he did not adequately reckon with the circumstances of his moment—circumstances to which I will turn later. It failed because of flaws in his vision that would become the themes of Hawthorne and Melville. It failed, I suppose, because all such projects fail. Does not this fatality form the very ground of his glory?

II

DISCIPLES
AND
CRITICS

TRUTHFULLY, are we to take seriously the annunciation of a new mankind by a small-town ex-minister who wrote obscure essays and lectured to miscellaneous audiences? Who tells us that currents of divinity flow through every soul, God being neither source nor end but the current itself? And this at a time when Andrew Jackson is grappling with the banks, the Abolitionists have declared war on slavery, and the country is preparing to tear itself apart?

Yet neither disciples nor opponents of Emerson would deny the lasting impress of his word. By summoning and then transcending an American sense of possibilities, he placed these before future generations, forever to lure and baffle. The evidence is simply ourselves. Norman Mailer writes that in America "a new kind of man was born from the idea that God was present in every man not only as compassion but as power." The painter Fairfield Porter tells us that he wanted to make of his pictures "a first experience in nature." Whether Mailer and Porter read Emerson matters little; Emerson had read them.

The embarrassment we may feel before Emerson's project is a sign of a provincialism that identifies all provincialisms except itself. Lock Emerson into our present littleness and he seems, to pygmy eyes, a pygmy. Place him in his historical moment or, if you prefer, in the spaces of eternity and you see why his influence, wax or wane, is unlikely ever to disappear in America.

His moment was one of those Gershom Scholem calls a "plastic hour." Possibility gleams. Men feel strengthened by an influx of powers, though Emerson would say those powers have always been there, waiting only to be released. My view of Emerson as a representative man of a privileged moment might not have pleased him, since he believed in the autonomy of spirit apart from mere conditions. He believed in it so ardently that he would have resisted such terms as "historical forces" and "structures of power"—terms that to us may be as real as lead but which to him were the merest specters of timidity. If you believe, as Emerson wrote, that man, indeed all being, is "pervaded by the nerves of God," you can dispense with historical method.

To whom was Emerson speaking in the 1830s and 1840s? To a few of his neighbors, like Bronson Alcott; to educated Americans who might drop in at his lectures; to all mankind. It is a mark of his imperturbability—a country patience, which sometimes can make one a little impatient—that he does not worry the matter of audience. He takes his time; the time is his. Lecturing in a flat and quiet voice, Emerson warned himself to say not what his audience expected to hear, but what was fit for him to say. Except when stung by the Unitarian hierarchs, he refrained from polemic: "argument burns up perception." Confident that his thought had an inner strength and would therefore outlast the pronouncements of the famous and powerful, he felt no need to worry about mass audiences. I find this almost enviable.

Emerson supposed it finally did not matter whether he reached all within his range or enabled one man, perhaps only himself, to achieve "self-union." A single example might ignite the world. Meanwhile he showed a touch of humor about himself, though humor is not usually his strong point. He had measured shrewdly enough the gap between desire and capacity:

> Far off, no doubt, is the perfectibility; so far off as to be ridiculous to all but a few. Yet wrote I once that God keeping a private door to each soul, nothing transcends the bounds of reasonable expectations from a man. Now what imperfect tad-

poles we are! . . . [Yet] who does not feel in him budding the powers of a Persuasion that by and by will be irresistible?

Whether or when those powers will break out, we cannot know. To envisage a democratization of the sublime—the essential Emersonian project—is to propose that all classes, groups, and even lumps can become self-reliant and autonomous, perhaps even flecked with divinity. All that stands in the way is habit, convention, fear, timidity. By the late 1840s Emerson might also have acknowledged the recalcitrance of those social institutions he had previously minimized.

An ardent disciple, Harold Bloom, tells us that Emerson "is more than prepared to give up on the great masses that constitute mankind. His hope . . . is that a small community of the spirit can come into existence." Now it is true you can find almost anything you want in Emerson's writings, and by, say, the 1850s he might have been ready to settle for a "small community of the spirit." Every democratic idealist, his goal not yet reached, must at times settle provisionally for something like that. But no democrat can give up "on the great masses" and remain a democrat; nor was this Emerson's intent during his early and most creative phase, the one Bloom rightly singles out as central to American culture.

In "The Poet" (1843) Emerson suggests that the poet stands not apart from or above other men, he stands *with* them. However uneasily, the poet stands "among partial men for the complete man, and apprises us not of his wealth, but of the commonwealth." Bearing gifts of perception, the poet celebrates the democratic ethos, "to turn the world into glass," a transparency of freedom. For American poets to come, Emerson did not make things easy.

Emerson's "Central Man," whose mission is surprise, might be anyone. I offer but two versions, as distant from each other as any could be. In an 1846 journal entry Emerson writes:

> The Poet should install himself & shove all usurpers from their chairs by electrifying mankind . . . The true centre thus appearing, all false centres are suddenly superseded, and grass grows in the Capitol.

Scholars usually stress the first sentence, but my political eye, the left one, trembles before that concluding clause: "grass grows in the Capitol." For this seems one of the few instances when, caution abandoned, Emerson yielded to a strain of native anarchism. The poet, "electrifying mankind," is to lead us all—and then, heavenly prospect, the state will wither away. Such a poet soon appeared; he sang of leaves of grass—but, alas, couldn't make any grow in the Capitol!

A second variant of "the Central Man" turns out to be a woman. Asked whether she understood an Emerson lecture, a washerwoman is reputed to have answered: "Not a word, but I like to see him stand up there and look as though he thought everyone was as good as he was." The multiple readings to which we can put "as good as he was" make this washerwoman a very princess of hermeneutics.

So everyone, anyone, or just this one could be the Emersonian audience; or when despair yielded to spectral Fate, no one at all.

Meanwhile there was the sustaining inner circle. Though Emerson wrote, "My doom and my strength is to be solitary," he managed rather well as the central figure or uncomfortable leader of an intellectual group, a loose assortment of speculators and seekers. (Hawthorne mocked them in his satiric fable "The Celestial Railroad," casting the ogre "Giant Transcendentalist" as "a heap of fog and duskiness," but that gassy "Giant" would leave a mark on Hawthorne's pages too.) In dealing with his colleagues, Emerson proved himself to be shrewder than he acknowledged to himself, and shrewder than biographers and scholars commonly allow. Because "insatiable" in his desire, he was not at all "greedy" in his reach, so that he could keep his allies at an optimal distance—close enough to inhale their musings, far enough to avoid clammy intrigues. If Thoreau did break past his guard for a time, it caused both of them an excess of pain. Perhaps it was sexual fright that led Emerson to disappoint Margaret Fuller, but he seems also to have sensed that in a little community of thinkers like the one he had put together, so volatile a spirit could wreak havoc. And he also knew that once an intellectual group hardens into a sect, the result can only be disaster.

Editing *The Dial,* Emerson showed similar crafts of management. A "little magazine" must be speculative, outlandish, prepared for the ridicule of proper Bostonians. Let it be open to the vaporous reflections of young Channing and Alcott, certainly to the green thoughts of Thoreau. Let it be experimental, "our poor little thing," which in its "first number," joked Emerson, "scarcely contains anything considerable or even visible." Sarah Clarke, a friend, said that "the spirit of many pieces" in *The Dial* "was lonely"—exactly what the spirit should be, otherwise why take on the burden of littleness? With its few hundred subscribers, *The Dial* set a precedent for *The Seven Arts, Hound and Horn,* and *Partisan Review.* It defined the role of the intellectual as critical, oppositional, even utopian, serving as the advocate of an avant-garde when there is one, but otherwise still saying "No," even if—New England being New England—not quite always in thunder.

Thoreau, closest of the disciples, outstripped Emerson now and again. Thoreau had a keener apprehension of the taste of experience—its sensuousness, if not sensuality—than Emerson did; he could enjoy the abundance of nature for its own sake, quite apart from any signals of spirit it gave off. Thoreau grasped more exactly the immediate guise of the alienation they both deplored: "The laboring man has not leisure for a true integrity day by day; he cannot afford to sustain the manliest relation to men; his labor would be depreciated in the market." He grasped more alertly than Emerson how a simulation of ritual might be used by a writer for compositional order. And though a less pungent aphorist, he had a better gift for narrative and exposition than Emerson did. Emerson's words are pebbles, Thoreau's can make a whole river-bed.

But if Thoreau sharpens the contours of Emersonian thought, he also coarsens its texture. *Walden* is a masterpiece as nothing of comparable length by Emerson can be said to be, but the thought behind *Walden* tends to be fixed into category, or at least posture, rarely turning back upon itself, as Emerson does in his journals, and almost never stumbling over a flaw, a gap, a doubt. The brilliance of Thoreau's prose shields a mind a little too content with itself. Emerson calls for a path to life; Thoreau offers a way of life. Disdaining the world, Thoreau strikes an attitude of truculence for its benefit, perhaps even for its amusement. He writes with the taunt of the virtuoso, often persuading us that his virtuosity is so remarkable we had better put up with his taunt. Emerson writes with the strain of a man struggling to extend his thought. Thoreau seems to offer answers to the problems of life—how we yearn for them!—but then, disappointed, we see that his answers are mostly literary. Perhaps a writer can provide no more, but I doubt it. Emerson doubted it too, as in his cutting note to, or about, Thoreau: "My dear Henry, A frog was made to live in a swamp, but a man was not made to live in a swamp. Yours ever."

For most of Thoreau's life he regarded freedom as an absolute state of being, which might be won through rituals of self-control and asceticism, after shaking off the torpor of convention. He was contemptuous, as Emerson usually was not, of those who saw freedom as a vulnerable arrangement between government and citizens requiring social constraints. Except possibly by way of preliminary, Thoreau's vision of freedom did not depend upon or require communal experience. At times he seemed to believe that sublimity can be sustained through austere exercises, a harsh stripping-down of life; Emerson, knowing better, saw the sublime as a gift of moments. Thinking as he did, Thoreau could fall into the rigidity of the fanatic, perhaps the crank. Emerson never did.*

This vision of freedom as an absolute state of being is a powerful vision, and it has its lasting value, especially for those who reject it out of an attachment to the rules and limits of a liberal society. Thoreau cared little about either rules or limits, and perhaps less about society; he proposed, with just a glint of cynicism, to accept the advantages society might offer while offering it no fealty. "A man more right than his neighbors constitutes a majority of one already," said Thoreau, without troubling to add—nor have those disciples who love this sentence troubled to explain—how that rightness is to be established or how competing claims to rightness, all of them, let us say, forceful and sincere, are to be adjudicated. Thoreau drives to an extreme a version of individualism that in later decades would lend itself to conservative bullying and radical posturing, both of which can undercut the fraternal basis of a democratic polity.

A master of English prose but sometimes just a terrific ranter, Thoreau can irritate by his programmed indifference to coherent argument in writings that bear an outer design of argument. Consider his late essay "Life Without Principle" (posthumously published, but an 1854 lecture) in which he displays formidable powers as a social critic:

---

*One entry in Emerson's journals for 1848 astonishes because of its harshness: "Henry Thoreau is like the woodgod who solicits the wandering poet & draws him into antres vast & desarts idle, & bereaves him of his memory, & leaves him naked, plaiting vines & with twigs in his hand. Very seductive are the first steps from the town to the woods, but the End is want & madness."

Many are ready to live by luck, and so get the means of commanding the labor of others less lucky, without contributing any value to society.

The ways by which you may get money almost without exception lead downward. To have done anything by which you earned money *merely* is to have been truly idle or worse. If the laborer gets no more than the wages which his employer pays him, he is cheated, he cheats himself. If you would get money as a writer or lecturer, you must be popular, which is to go down perpendicularly.

We must always cherish a writer capable of that splendid "perpendicularly"; but how are we to relate such reflections to Thoreau's insistence in the same essay that "my connection with and obligations to society are still very slight and transient?" This strikes me as being close to mere pose. A man with "very slight and transient" connections to society would not be able, nor would he take the trouble, to write with such critical acuteness about it. Thoreau seems to have clung to a rigid theoretical individualism—a posture—long after he came to live by more generous and complex values. Only seldom was his thought a match for his perceptions.

If I have been unfair to Thoreau, it is because I have meant to be unfair. His prose I would emulate if I could, but his intellectual style seems to me troubling, sometimes repellent. Emerson acknowledges the fissures of the soul, the "two" which rarely fuse into "one," while Thoreau would present himself as utterly armored, a martial figure without chink or weakness. Thoreau, the greater artist, has that coldness of voice T. S. Eliot thought characteristic of true writers; but he is the lesser thinker, the poorer model, a marginal variant, if one at all, of "the Central Man."

Thoreau takes Emerson's thought, finally, to lock it in. Whitman, less bedazzled by definition, floats through a series of selves in both life and poetry, musing, yielding to all but none entirely. There is a strange passiveness in Whitman, at its loveliest in his murmuring solitariness ("Only the lull I like, the hum of your valvèd voice"). That murmur sounds to me oddly like Melville's in depicting his plebeian hero Ishmael, wonderfully chaste when compared to the barking assertiveness of the national character. In this state of receptivity Whitman takes everything in: the carnival of politics, the vulgarity of chauvinism, the sweetness of fraternity, the puzzlement of selfhood, the comedy of a culture supposing it had in reserve an endless repertoire of acts, skits, and parts, each fitting the self. Drifting from persona to persona, tableau to tableau, Whitman assimilates it all with amusement but also criticism, reminding Americans that death will reach them too, coming always on time—no matter how imperial or expansive their selves—to complete and dissolve being. As with Emerson, there lurks in Whitman a native skeptic: also a deviant, a bohemian, a furtive stranger from the streets. No wonder he both enchanted and alarmed Emerson, who saw that Whitman's verses, while realizing a democratized sublime that favored both work and loafing, also took this vision to precincts he, Emerson, could not approach: to alleyways and cellars, boardinghouses and military hospitals. The risk in democratizing the sublime is that you may lose a quadrant of sublimity.

Whitman carries the Emersonian vision into new settings, new terms of history—if not yet the industrial city, then the commercial city of mobs, toughs, loners, stragglers, and strangers. Of all these, Emerson was acquainted only with loners. Whitman's city can still flourish in a hypothetical union with surrounding green; there is, still, a portion of Emersonian roominess, so that this Brooklyn bohemian exalting the masses can knock about on his own, a new world flaneur, without feeling overwhelmed. Society for Whitman was not so claustrophobic as it is for us; but it was more provisioned and substantial than for Emerson. In *Leaves of Grass* the city seems a secondary presence, only on occasion blocking desire in the way we have come to expect. So while Whitman leaves behind, as any New Yorker would have to, Emerson's cool sense of separateness, he finds convenient Emersonian angles of vision when looking upon the world of commerce and labor. Whitman still aspires to satisfy Emerson's prescription that the American poet evoke the new democratic man, less perhaps through exalted vision than a rotation of possibilities; but he does not locate "the Central Man" at the center. Anticipating the strategies, or losses, of later American writers, he locates that urgent figment in the crevices of a world changing too quickly for him, or anyone else, fully to grasp.

Even with such disciples of genius, the Emersonian vision turns out to be flitting, elusive—perhaps because it is delusional to suppose that a new country has to give rise to a new mankind; perhaps because the favorable American setting which was Emerson's tacit premise was being swept away by history; perhaps because a project of this kind, though never to be abandoned, is never to be completed. Meanwhile, a novelist skeptical of all visions, the Emersonian one most of all, provides the first persuasive portrait of Emerson's new American: a woman named Hester Prynne who, if not quite "a seeker with no Past at my back," stands ready to pay the price for her self-reliant assertions.

Of the many Emersons—some will never make it to these pages—one of the keenest is the social observer who describes the rebellious youth of his day. It is "a sign of the times" that "intelligent and religious persons" withdraw from common life and "betake themselves to a certain solitary and critical way of living, from which no solid fruit has yet appeared to justify their separation." Had anyone before Emerson noticed, with so nice a balance of the amiable and caustic, this recurrent aspect of American life? Had anyone before him had reason to notice? "They are striking work, and crying out for something worthy to do"—a quiet sentence that renews itself each time America turns from money to value. Emerson continues in the same kindly, needling way:

> They are not good citizens . . . They do not even like to vote. The philanthropists [reformers] inquire whether Transcendentalism does not mean sloth; they had as lief hear that their friend is dead, as that he is a Transcendentalist; for then he is paralyzed, and can never do anything for humanity.

An ironic reversal follows:

> Society also has its duties in reference to this class [For there might, after all] be room for the exciters and monitors; collectors of the heavenly spark.

A time of reforming zeal brings a clutter of cranks, fanatics, and bores. In the years of "the newness" there were fanatics, despots of conscience, for whom any political compromise seemed the work of the devil. There were cranks who thought converse with the ordinary world a stain of corruption. Figures of this kind had been memorably sketched by William Hazlitt:

> About the time of the French Revolution, it was agreed that the world had hitherto been in its dotage or its infancy; . . . The past had neither thought nor object worthy to arrest our attention; and the future would be equally a senseless void, except as we projected ourselves and our theories into it.

Kindlier than Hazlitt, Emerson took a kindlier view, perhaps because he had to, the celebrant of the inner voice not always being certain which among the many voices deserved notice. The shrewd Yankee jostling the Oversoul in Emerson's frame knew that in reform movements wastage is part of till-age. Nevertheless, one marvels at Emerson's good humor. The world seemed roomier in his day; deviants could find their little margin and writers abide the fantastical. Even when reporting the Chardon Street convention, that circus of perfectibility, Emerson saw some value in social fantasy. While defending the reformers, he also wrote—I employ a suggestive anachronism—in a social democratic spirit, urging them to a discrimination among goals:

> It is the part of a fanatic to fight out a revolution on the shape of a hat or surplice, on paedo-baptism or altar-rails or fish on Friday . . . wait until you have a good difference to join issue upon. Thus Socrates was told he should not teach. "Please God, but I will." And he could die well for that. And Jesus had a cause. You [too] will get one by and by.

Moral revolutionists dreaming of "the perfectibility" can be shrewd tacticians.

But enough of this, cry the world's practical men. Tell us: What *was* Emerson's word? So asked, the question cannot be answered. Revolutionist without revolution, reformer without reforms, prophet without... To be sure, Emerson exalted consciousness, but how much weight are we to allow sheer consciousness? Can it be the all of life?

The suspicion that Emerson thinks so makes one uneasy. There are moments when he seems intent upon making consciousness the beginning and end of existence, a vast enclosure in which the self roams about, monarch of its substance, swallowing the very world in its pride and yielding readily to sublime dissolution. Consciousness, assimilating everything, is to serve as a light not upon experience but upon itself. This view of things would be taken to an extreme by Henry James when he proposed to enlarge "the field of consciousness fur-

ther and further, making it lose itself in the ineffable"—
though his story "The Beast in the Jungle" can be read as a
strong counterthrust, an instance of a writer brilliantly savag-
ing his own premises. Perhaps this imperial consciousness is
what T. S. Eliot had in mind when he said New England was
"refined beyond the point of civilization."

The exasperated questions persist: what does Emerson propose? what does he want?

Realists of liberalism applaud the Emerson of the 1850s,
once he joined publicly in the battle against slavery. Realists of
conservatism see him as a noble fantasist who in middle age
parachuted to earth. Realists of radicalism keep reminding
him that deep changes in character are conditional upon deep
changes in social relations. Emerson barely heeds the lot of
them. Insisting that the liberation of consciousness is the work
of consciousness alone, he puts his wager on a generation of
"Young Americans" and teaches himself to wait. His special
parish, as he nicely puts it, is young men inquiring their way of
life.

His terms are unlikely to satisfy those of us who live, or
would live, in the public realm. Consider some of his key
words. "Power"—the exercise of a universal potential, but
also, as if in contradiction, the lordly prerogatives of the hero.
"Self-union"—a healing into oneness, a closing with divinity.
"Eloquence"—"in perfect eloquence, the hearer would lose the
sense of dualism." (But the mind might lose a capacity for
criticism.) "Sublime"—that moment of spiritual elevation
which now, grandly egalitarian, is to affirm the radiance of all
creatures. "Self-reliance"—finally Emerson's key term, with
the Enlightenment, romanticism, and republicanism joining
to proclaim a new presence in history, that active conquering
"self" which we now suppose our natural possession but
which is actually a hypothesis won through historical struggle. "Self-reliance" as guide and value brings us to a central

difficulty in Emersonian thought: the tendency to reduce it to individualism as ideology; or, put another way, the tendency toward a tragic sundering between democratic sentiment and individualist aggrandizement.

Emerson refuses a program. He hesitates to draw the features of "the Central Man" for reasons similar to those that led Marx to reject blueprints for the socialist future. If you can describe the newness, then it may not be new. But if you refuse to try, then there is little you can say about it except that it is new.

Emerson tries to escape this difficulty through metaphor, invocation, poetry:

> Heaven walks among us ordinarily muffled in such triple or tenfold disguises that the wise are deceived and no one suspects the days to be gods.

> Recognize "the days to be gods" and man may "become as large as nature."

What does Emerson propose? What does he want? He proposes almost nothing and wants almost everything—"as large as nature."

The Emersonian outlook is open to historical criticism, but for the moment let us consider it as what might be called a philosophical anthropology. Is there not something unsatisfying in that view of human experience which proposes an all-but-absolute self-sufficiency of each individual and makes "self-reliance" the primary value? Something deeply impoverishing in the linked view that contents itself with individualism as ideology? To exalt what Steven Lukes calls "the Abstract Individual," one who consists "merely in a certain set of invariant psychological characteristics and tendencies," which in popular thought become fixed into a "human nature" largely unaffected by historical change—to do this is to suppress life's complexities, possibilities, dangers, and, most of all, necessary entanglements. As F. H. Bradley writes, with a fine sweep:

> the "individual" apart from the community is an abstraction . . . I am myself by sharing with others, by including in my essence relations to them . . . If I wish to realize my true being, I must therefore realize something beyond my being as mere this or that; for my true being has in it a life which is not the life of any particular, and so must be called a universal life.

Place next to Bradley's idealist passage a materialist observation by Marx:

> Since [the individual of the bourgeois era] appeared to be in conformity with nature . . . he was regarded not as a product of history, but of nature. This illusion has been characteristic of every new epoch in the past.

Bradley's passage has its bearing since it starts from terms close to Emerson's ("realize my true being") but ends at a point quite distant. (Emerson would have agreed that "my true being has in it a life which is not the life of any particular," but I think he would have balked at "including in my essence relations to [others]," since his sense of "sharing" extended far more readily to the universe at large than to particular men and women.) And the passage from Marx is to the point because it helps place historically—in a way Emerson would probably have refused—the Emersonian individual as a figure or product of "every new epoch." If Bradley's criticism is strong, Marx's placement is shrewd.

The individual as a type, and individualism as an idea or ideology, are historical developments, social constructs, not fixed and immutable, apart from time and circumstance. The individual is a *creation* of mankind, and it is possible to suggest with fair precision when he first appeared. The moral, psychological, and social attributes of this individual vary sharply from place and moment to place and moment. Just as the figure of the individual takes shape and coloration from social introjection, so the idea or ideology of individualism can be—and has been—put to a bewildering variety of uses.

Yet if the Emersonian anthropology can be shaken by historical criticism, so can the criticism itself. We have, toward the end of the twentieth century, good reason to hesitate. The experience of our century both underscores the inadequacies of an absolutist individualism and the dangers of too sweeping an attack upon it. As against Bradley and Marx, consider the words of Isaiah Berlin, surely no Emersonian but at this point to be invoked as Emerson's partial ally:

> I wish my life and decisions to depend on myself, not on external forces of whatever kind. I wish to be the instrument of my own, not other men's acts of will . . . I wish to be . . . self-directed and not acted upon by external nature or by other men.

Two apparently irreconcilable visions of life seem locked in opposition, and Emerson looks on, bemused at our twisting and turning, though still insisting that the liberation of consciousness is the work of consciousness alone. If we do not yield him full accord, then at least we may allow him a new and wary respect. If we are at a standstill, a standstill is precisely where we should be, hoping for some miraculous balance, which we know to be unavailable, between rival claims. How are we to make the "two" of experience melt into the "one" for which thought hungers? All we can do is initiate an act of desire, and I propose to do that, not with argument, but in a perhaps more powerful way: anecdote.

In Rashi's Commentaries on the Pentateuch he quotes the verse: "And the Lord appeared to [Abraham] by the terebinths of Memre, as he sat in the tent door in the heat of the day." After which Rashi offers this lovely story:

God came down to visit the sick. Rabbi Hama ben Hanina said that on the third day after Abraham's circumcision, God came to inquire after his health. Why was Abraham sitting at the tent door? To see if there were any travelers whom he could invite into his home. The verse describes the incident as taking place in the heat of the day. On this phrase the Talmud notes that God brought out the sun so that Abraham would not be troubled by any passers-by. But then God saw that Abraham was grieved at the absence of visitors, so He sent him the angels in the guise of men.

And here is an anecdote in which the Italian writer Ignazio Silone remembers an incident from childhood. He saw, in front of his house, a "pitiful, farcical sight," a little man, a prisoner, being dragged away by two enormous policemen.

"Look how funny he is," I said to [my father] with a laugh.

My father looked severely at me, dragged me to my feet by the ear and led me to his room. I had never seen him so angry at me.

"What have I done wrong," I asked him, rubbing my injured ear.

"Never make fun of a man who's been arrested! Never!"

"Why not?"

"Because he can't defend himself. And because he may be innocent. In any case, because he's unhappy."

It would be unjust to think that Emerson would not have been touched by these stories, or the ideas behind them, quite as much as we are. But it does seem fair to suggest that, with their evocation of such values as sociability and solidarity, these are not the kinds of stories he would have been likely to tell—one of his strange flaws is an indifference to stories in general. The stories from Rashi and Silone stress a sharing of travail that Melville would call "the universal thump" but which the cult of self-reliance is ill-equipped to grasp.

Perceptions of this order control the fiction of Hawthorne and Melville. In Hawthorne's brilliant early story "My Kinsman, Major Molineaux," there is an oblique but sharp criticism of that opportunistic aggrandizement which is often set free by the ethos of individualism. Whether Hawthorne so intended the story, I cannot say; but I am convinced that the customary reading, such as James Mellow's judgment that this "is a conventional story of initiation, of the rites of passage and the topping of a familiar authority," goes askew. The external scheme of the story is that of initiation; it can also be read as a sour celebration of the American democracy's triumph over aristocratic Britain; but as often with Hawthorne, inner content breaks past outer shell.

A "shrewd" youth from the country, Robin Molineaux, comes to town in search of his powerful kinsman, Major Molineaux. The time is pre-Revolutionary; the major serves the British king; the youth has no discernible opinions. In a series of hallucinatory encounters, he meets a devil-like figure, his face half-black, half-red; a winsome harlot in scarlet petticoat; an elder who threatens to put him in the stocks; and an amiable gentleman—forerunner of certain smoothies in *The Confidence Man*—who comforts the confused yet "shrewd" youth by telling him that soon he will be seeing his kinsman, Major Molineaux.

Suddenly a parade, a howling mob, and in its midst, a prisoner, Major Molineaux, in "tar-and-feather dignity." The description of the Major is positive: he is "of large and majestic person, and [has] strong, square features, betokening a steady soul." At the height of his ordeal he is "majestic still." The only unworthy thing we know about him is that he is on the "wrong," the British, side. As the mob howls, Robin feels at first the classical response of "pity and terror," but he is not the sort to remain loyal to a mere victim. Apparently untroubled by sentiments of kinship or fellow-feeling, he joins the mob in its "contagion" of laughter. Note the word "contagion"; also Hawthorne's characterization of the mob, "like fiends that throng in mockery round some dead potentate." Hardly language for paragons of liberty.

At the end our "shrewd" youth decides that, his chance for advancement over with, he might as well go back to the country. But no; the amiable gentleman, cheerleader for the mob, tells him to remain, for so "shrewd" a youth "may rise in the world without the help of your kinsman, Major Molineaux."

I have kept repeating the adjective "shrewd," though not so often as Hawthorne does, eleven times by my count. This repetition ought to have alerted critics that he is not exactly enraptured with Robin as representative of rural virtue or burgeoning democracy. Endlessly sly, Hawthorne entraps his readers by seeming to align the historical pattern of the story with its moral detail, but finally he makes the two into blunt antagonists. We have been set up for a patriotic response: numerous critics declare Robin to be a rough but worthy agent of the young democracy. But if we attend Hawthorne's language, we see that it elicits, at the very least, an unnerving skepticism. Robin turns out to have an eye, not exactly unknown in the countryside, for the main chance. He does not become "shrewd" upon entering the city; he already *is* "shrewd" upon his arrival—otherwise, he is not likely to have come to the city in the first place. He needs little help in the arts of opportunism: we may be confident of his success. Without troubling to make any judgment about the fate of his kinsman, he slides into the camp of tar-and-feather. That, after all, is where his future lies, where a "shrewd" youth belongs.

Robin's individualism is that of low cunning. A more elevated version, but also a deeper moral criticism, is to be found in *Moby-Dick*. Melville's book dramatizes, with a classical ex-

actness, the split between democratic fraternity and aggrandiz-
ing individualism. Sharing some of the premises and much of
the aspiration of the Emersonian ethos, it ends with a profound, yet not quite dissociative, criticism.

Ishmael and Ahab are not merely counterposed as fictional
characters, they represent sharply divergent spiritual styles.
Ishmael proposes to open himself to the possibilities of life,
the illuminations of strangers, even cannibals; Ahab has locked
his mind into a single purpose and plans to bend the whole of
the *Pequod* to it. Ishmael yearns for identity, "self-union";
Ahab lusts after the powers of abstraction. About Ishmael
there is nothing heroic, and that is one reason to love him;
about Ahab there is a warped, awesome grandeur, and we
have almost no choice but to admire and fear him. Ishmael
seeks to reenter Hawthorne's "magnetic chain of humanity";
Ahab, in the mania of pure ends, would make that chain a
device for enslaving his men. Ishmael's goodness is that he can
learn; Ahab's magnificence, a refusal to learn. To those who
say that democracy must foster mediocrity, Ishmael is one
answer—an enlarging humane modesty; Ahab another answer—that democracy can bring forth powers worse than
mediocrity.

Overcoming the drizzly November of his soul, Ishmael es-
tablishes a friendship with Queequeg, a plebeian brotherhood
murmuringly honored. It is the most beautiful spirit this
country has ever evoked, and later it will subside into the quiet
deliberateness of shared work on board ship. But on board
that ship, Ahab the fanatic seeker rules. Here will is all. Some
critics have seen Ahab as agent of bourgeois expansion, but
surely this is a mistake; he scorns that spirit as petty, ignoble;
he cares nothing about whale oil or dollars. What might, at
most, be true is that the ruthlessness of will he has put to
metaphysical ends could also be turned to bourgeois ac-
cumulation.

Ahab is a brilliant madman, intent upon a goal that has overcome him, reducing him to its agent, but also lending him the force with which to break his men into submission. They submit to the thrill of purpose. Their readiness to do so is a terrifying aspect of the book, perhaps uncovering a weakness inherent in the democratic enterprise. A little Ahabism in the men Ahab conquers might be a sufficient obstacle to Ahab. The one figure who could have overruled him is the handsome sailor Bulkington, noble defender of the plebes. But Melville, with a six-inch obituary, dispatches him to the sea, as if again perhaps to indicate how fragile are popular defenses against the contagion of that charismatic demonism which both bedevils and ennobles Ahab. Certainly the Christian humanism of Starbuck cannot stop Ahab. Nor can the secular fraternity of Ishmael and his co-workers—which may be one reason that for long stretches of the book Ishmael simply disappears. He has in himself no potential for significant action.

Were Melville not ambivalent toward Ahab, there would be neither a book nor a problem. He wants us to admire the grandeur of Ahab's obsession, yet to back away from its excesses. Ahab must control, must know, must grasp, the heart of things. And if there is none? Then he must know that. This hunger for knowledge-as-control has a retributive aspect, not only because Ahab has lost a leg to the whale, but because he understands, dimly, how hopeless are the odds in the battle between man and the wish to overcome cosmic ignorance. Ahab magnifies and debases the Emersonian notion of "power." Instead of sharing in divinity, he would imprison it. If Melville is a semi-disciple of Emerson, he is the kind who plunges a knife into the master's weakest spot.

Ahab wants to penetrate the nature of nature. Ishmael abides with consciousness, the rich expanding consciousness of the book as it seeks an unsigned accord with the world in which consciousness must exist—this means, partly, a fraternity with all races and colors of men and, partly, a precarious equilibrium with an alien nature. Is this the Emersonian democratic sublime? I am not sure. The exquisite passages in which Ishmael and Queequeg establish their brotherhood speak for a democracy of ease, a union of the plebes, but they are not quite so grand or transcendent as the word "sublime" would suggest. I take the experience of Ishmael and Queequeg to be secular. An inverted sublimity is reserved for Ahab, perhaps because he, a crippled Yankee metaphysician still engaged with nature, reaches moments of elevation without nobility, epic grandeur without tragic grasp. Indeed, to reach the grandeur, he must choose to deny himself the grasp.

If there is any truth in these remarks, then I must retract some of my earlier criticisms of Emerson's attitude regarding consciousness. For here, in Melville's quieter pages, consciousness can become a mode of learning, an inducement to humility, perhaps an aid to survival. It is the conqueror Ahab who imprisons knowledge; Ishmael, the man of consciousness, abides with it, allotting a just share to I and a just share to Thou.

History gave Emerson his opportunity; history took it away. Within a few years the Emersonian project would be overwhelmed by the peculiarly rapid pace of social change in America.

The lingering past—accursed slavery; the troublesome present—a democratic politics increasingly vulgarized; the future—a new industrial civilization calling into question the Emersonian categories. All converge within a few decades. To cope with all three would have taken a genius beyond Emerson's, perhaps beyond anyone's. By the 1840s slavery had broken into Emerson's calm, troubling his dreams, agitating his consciousness, forcing him into the commonplace world of politics, reform, compromise. Perhaps even earlier he had been roused to a deep repugnance toward the politics of the young republic: what sensitive person born while Jefferson and Adams were still alive could bear the thought of Polk and Pierce? Emerson was experiencing the rise of politics as mass culture, a phenomenon we have lived to see in its full beauty. He did not like it; the whig in him being repelled, the democrat dismayed. He would give way at times to a kind of republican elitism, that claim to represent some higher national value as against sectional or class or, as we now say, "special" interests—a strategy of high-minded Americans often masking conservative inclinations with a sheen of rectitude.

Then, as the most familiar and fundamental of the historical experiences to overwhelm Emerson, came a new economy, a new society, a new rhythm of labor, a new pattern of exploitation, a new calculus of profit. What could Emerson make of it as he approached old age? What could he make of robber barons, multimillionaires, vast factories with regiments of laborers, corporations, strikes and lockouts, industrial violence, hordes of immigrants speaking scores of tongues, in short the world that has made us? Almost desperately he pleads against the growing concern with "the masses," those who, he says unsympathetically but not stupidly, "are rude, lame, unmade," who "need not to be flattered, but to be schooled." He wished to "break them up, and draw individuals out of them." Very good; but what Emerson could not see—and who can blame him?—was that in this new industrial world the conditions of life were such that for these rude "masses" the path to individual definition often lay through collective action, that the factory worker could assert himself as a man only by joining in common action with his fellow workers and thereby creating at least the possibility of personality. Emerson was by no means lacking in gifts of dialectic, but this far he could not drive them.

His vision broke—or, rather, split—and became subject to a wide range of purposes. It could show forth the Emerson who, in behalf of a perfect unfolding of individual nature, analyzed human alienation in a commercial society, attacking the invasion of "Nature by Trade . . . [as it threatened] to upset the balance of man, and establish a new, universal Monarchy more tyrannical than Babylon or Rome." And it could emerge in the Emerson who told his countrymen that "money . . . is in its effects and laws as beautiful as roses. Property keeps the accounts of the world, and is always moral." His vision of American possibility could coexist with Daniel Webster and inspire Wendell Phillips. It could be exploited by Social Darwinism and sustain Abolitionism. It could veer toward an American anarchism, suspicious of all laws, forms, and regulations, while also tilting rightward toward worship of the "free market." Snakelike, it could subside next to the Lockean moderation of the makers of the Constitution. Rising up from the recesses of the American imagination, it resembles Freud's description of dreams as showing "a special tendency to reduce two opposites to a unity or to represent them as one thing."

This last criticism of the Emersonian world view—that it was ill-equipped to confront the problems of an industrial society—may seem distinctively modern, but it had been advanced as early as 1840 by the gifted and erratic New England writer Orestes Brownson. Influenced by French utopian socialists, Brownson wrote a remarkable proto-Marxist essay called "The Laboring Classes," which among other things is a tacit polemic against Emerson, perhaps most of all in its insistence that society constitutes a distinct realm of human activity not reducible to the sum of individual wills. Reformers, Brownson writes:

would have all men wise, good, and happy; but in order to make them so, they tell us that we want not external changes, but internal; and therefore instead of seeking to disturb existing social arrangements, we should confine ourselves to the individual reason and conscience [so as] to seek . . . [the] reformation of life . . .

This is doubtless a capital theory, and has the advantage that kings, hierarchies, nobilities . . . will feel no difficulty in supporting it . . . If you will only allow me to keep thousands toiling for my pleasure or my profit, I will even aid you in your pious efforts to convert their souls.

Brownson proceeds to a direct thrust at Emerson:

Self-culture is a good thing, but it cannot abolish inequality, nor restore men to their rights. As a means of quickening moral and intellectual energy . . . and preparing the laborer to contend manfully for his rights, we admit its importance . . . but as constituting in itself a remedy for the vices of the social state we have no faith in it . . .

The truth is, the evil we have pointed out is not merely individual in character . . . What is purely individual in its nature, efforts of individuals to perfect themselves may remove. But the evil we speak of is inherent in all our social arrangements, and cannot be cured without a radical change of those arrangements.

In the years since Brownson wrote his essay our sense of historical dialectic has been sharpened by witnessing "a radical change of [social] arrangements," which, however, brought neither greater freedom nor relief for the laboring classes. We are now inclined to reject a simple dichotomy between social transformation and individual regeneration; we insist, perhaps with a fashionable quotation from Gramsci, upon their interdependence.

Brownson's attack on Emerson would be repeated later by such writers as John Jay Chapman, Van Wyck Brooks, and Newton Arvin. The argument is not quite so definitive as they supposed, for had Emerson chosen to, he might have made a cogent reply. He might have said that American society before the Civil War had not yet hardened to the extent Brownson assumed: there was still room for people to move and to grow. He might have said—but this he did say—that "each 'cause' . . . becomes speedily a little shop, where the article, let it have been at first ever so subtle . . . is now made up into portable and convenient cakes, and retailed in small quantities to suit purchasers." And he might have said that without the transformed individuals he desired, the movements Brownson was calling into existence were likely to sink into pettiness and corruption.

What gives Brownson's critique a special interest today is that it fits nicely with a recent trend in American historiography. A new school of young historians has drawn upon the thought of J. G. A. Pocock, who in *The Machiavellian Moment*, a work of erudition, has isolated a strand of political thought, flowing from the Italian Renaissance through England and into America, which he calls "republicanism."

The classical republic postulates an "individual as civic and active being, directly participating in the *respublica* according to his measure." By contrast, liberalism "appears as conscious chiefly of his interest and takes part in government in order to press for its realization." Even in the early republic there was already a fear that "virtue" would be replaced by "corruption," *homo politicus* by the regional or class brokers, and the republic by empire. "There is thus a dimension of historical pessimism in American thought at its most utopian, which stems from the confrontation of virtue and commerce."

Pocock's analysis, far more complex than I can summarize here, may lead to a certain modification in describing the Emersonian project. Perhaps it should now be seen not only as a hope or vision for fulfilling the promise of the American revolution but also as expressing a fear that the republic might be "corrupted" by forces it had itself set loose.

A recent historical study, Sean Wilentz's *Chants Democratic*, has taken over this notion of republicanism and tried to give it social, or class, body by examining the embryonic trade unions and workingmen's parties in New York during the 1820s and 1830s. Wilentz speaks of "artisan republicanism" as an early form of American radicalism, with virtue, independence, and so on being invoked by these movements in behalf of plebeian interests. Valuable as such historical studies are, especially insofar as they dissolve comforting fantasies about the United States as a classless society, they tend to exaggerate the importance of what they discover. In the sweep of pre–Civil War America, "artisan republicanism" and its isolated spokesmen could play only a marginal and transient role. By contrast, republicanism as a diffused political and cultural sentiment, not located in or confined to any particular class, seems to have been far more consequential. Emerson apparently knew little and wrote nothing about the rebellious movements in New York. To have given them any prominence in his thought would have been to jeopardize the project of his early years, which rested on the assumption that internal divisions in the country were not so serious as to impede the creation or appearance of "the Central Man." Yet republicanism as a social premise, as part of what had made the American Revolution and could now be brought to moral fulfillment, seems to have been shared intuitively by the early Emerson.

Precisely because Brownson's critique may strike us as cogent and up-to-date, we must conclude it was of only marginal significance in its own day. He was trying to battle—the odds were hopeless—against a pervasive but intuitive republican sentiment, indifferent to matters of class, upon which Emerson drew. He was insisting, with about as much success as later American socialists, upon the primacy of class divisions in American society. I think he showed remarkable foresight, but what finally mattered in the decades before the Civil War was not so much Brownson's critical prescience as Emerson's representative word—and Garrison's decisive acts. Irascible genius that he was, Brownson suffered what Engels has described as the tragedy of social analysts and movements that come too soon. If by now we recognize the strength of Brownson's critique, the irony is that in his own day Emerson could evade it almost unscathed.

Emerson was torn by the familiar choice between the claims of the mind and the claims of the world, but putting it this way may not be wholly to the point, since Emerson did not see his chosen path as that of the scholarly recluse. He believed, or so I am claiming, that his intellectual work was of this world and could, sooner or later, have a profound impact on this world. His problem was to adjudicate between two *kinds* of commitment, and that problem was not made easier by the fact that the reformers, many of them admirers and friends, were inclined to reduce the issue to a choice between scholarly retirement and public activity.

With Brook Farm his difficulties were relatively minor. When George Ripley and his friends sent their prospectus to Emerson, inviting him to join the colony, his response was firm: "I am in many respects suitably placed, in an agreeable neighborhood, in a town which I have many reasons to love, & which has respected my freedom so far that I presume it will indulge me farther if I need it." In his journal he was harsher:

> I do not wish to remove from my present prison ["a town which I have many reasons to love"?] to a prison a little larger. I wish to break all prisons. [I would not] hide my impotency in the thick of a crowd . . . Moreover, to join this body would be to

traverse all my long trumpeted theory . . . that one man is a counterpoise to a city . . . that his solitude is more prevalent & beneficial than the concert of crowds.

Emerson, I think, was right not to go to Brook Farm, even though I would align myself far more than he did with the party of social action. Utopian colonies become credible under two main conditions: when the life of a society has become so intolerable that decent humanity must find a way to insulate itself; and when spirited reformers intend to use the colony as a training school from which to embark upon their mission. But Emerson, reasonably enough, did not believe either of these conditions held true at the time Brook Farm was started; he looked upon it as a sort of indulgence by good but distracted people. Still, there is something touching in the way he agonized over Ripley's invitation: was he being merely prudent in refusing to join the experiment, merely self-protective? He might have said, what was true, that he was quite unsuited for such a place—just as today there are socialists, among whom I number, who would have to be driven at gunpoint before they would enter a commune, their hopes for a better world stopping short of the claustrophobic littleness of such colonies. Emerson understood that, apart from providing social amusements, such colonies would do little more than lump together, unmanageably, the problems of life which had originally led the colonists to coalesce. He understood that a colony like Brook Farm could not escape the society enclosing it—indeed, *was* the society enclosing it. But it was Hawthorne (again!) who best phrased the fatal limitations of such enterprises when in *The Blithedale Romance,* with language almost Marxist, he noted that, "as regarded society at large, we stood in a position of new hostility, rather than new brotherhood . . . We were inevitably estranged from the rest of mankind in pretty fair proportion with the strictness of our mutual bond among ourselves."

Emerson, friendly to the utopians, did not join Brook Farm; Hawthorne, skeptical about their ideas, did. How explain this? Hawthorne's biographers have kept repeating that he went to Brook Farm in order to straighten out his financial affairs before marriage. This turns Hawthorne into something of a dolt: who in his right mind could have supposed Brook Farm would help anyone financially? It also fails to probe beneath Hawthorne's explanation.

Needing the isolation under which he chafed, Hawthorne reveals in all his writings the deep pull of that "circle of humanity" which we would now call community. Writers dramatize most powerfully elements they sense to be lacking in themselves. Throughout his brief stay at Brook Farm, Hawthorne expressed his doubts in letters to his family and future wife, yet *he* had gone there, to shovel manure during the day and share meals, perhaps even conversation, in the evenings. It was a plunge into experience, of a sort; a plunge into that circle of kinship he could neither endure nor dismiss. And it was Hawthorne, the skeptic, who would write that the utopian experience expressed a yearning "a young man had better never have been born than not to have, and a mature man had better die at once than utterly to relinquish." Interestingly enough, this thought would be echoed by the elderly Emerson in his 1866 journal: Brook Farm was an experience, he wrote, "of life-long value . . . What knowledge of themselves & of each other . . . what personal power, what studies of character, what accumulated culture many of the members must have owed to it!"

It was with regard to the Abolitionists that Emerson found himself in a really profound inner struggle, one that kept recurring over the years. Again he had to face the question and, knowing the cause of Abolitionism to be essentially just, face it with a mounting anxiety: Could a man like himself live by the claims of spirit or must he acknowledge the claims of a fallen world? It was not a decision to be made through reflection alone or intuition alone, for "the moral sense" that kept plaguing him seemed to have taken on an autonomous life virtually apart from either reflection or intuition, and it drove him mercilessly to the burden of public duty. "The greatest saints," John Jay Chapman would write, "lived without an understanding of Abolition till, suddenly one day, Abolition broke out in their hearts and made them miserable." This misery we call conscience. Yet Emerson kept rationalizing and equivocating. There were ways in which he was no better than you or I.

How painful this inner conflict was can be seen in the contrast between two passages from his journals, written about a year apart during the early 1850s. The first is a stirring denunciation of the Fugitive Slave Law:

And this filthy enactment was made in the 19th Century, by people who could read and write. I will not obey it, by God.

The second is notorious:

I waked at night, and bemoaned myself, because I had not thrown myself into this deplorable question of Slavery . . . But then, in hours of sanity, I recover myself and say, God must govern his own world . . . without my desertion of my post which has none to guard it but me. I have quite other slaves to free than those negroes, to wit, imprisoned spirits, imprisoned thoughts, far back in the brain of man.

If there is one place where Emerson is open to a sharp moral judgment, it is here. It may be, as some admirers suggest, that he is rehearsing the familiar conflict, experienced by many writers, between personal interest and social conscience. But there is something sadly disingenuous—the writhing of a man who suspects he is in the wrong—when he uses language to suggest an equivalence, or even similarity, between "slave"

meaning shackled men and women and "slave" referring to
undeveloped thoughts and spirits.

About a year later Emerson returned to the slavery question, this time to attack the very Abolitionists he admired. He
subjected Wendell Phillips to a kind of criticism which in our
time would be made familiar by Lionel Trilling in his writings
about "the liberal imagination":

> Very dangerous is this thoroughly social & related life, whether
> antagonistic or co-operative. In a lonely world, or a world with
> half a dozen inhabitants, these would find nothing to do. The
> first discovery I made of Phillips, was, that while I admired his
> eloquence, I had not the faintest wish to meet the man. He had
> only a *platform*-existence, & no personality.

Well, perhaps. But let us think about this for a moment. I
have known, in my own periodic involvements, valuable people who, it may be, had "only a platform-existence." Or, more
humbly put, who seemed to. What Emerson said about Phillips might, from a distance, be said about Norman Thomas.
But in this world of wretchedness, where men like Phillips and
Thomas are always in short supply, is Emerson's charge really
so damning? When Phillips stood up against a lynch mob,
didn't he show as much self-reliance as Thoreau subsisting on
several and a half pennies in his hut?*

Soon enough Emerson would come back to Phillips, saying
the Abolitionist had "the supreme merit in this time, that
he and he alone stands in the gap." A fine tribute, but it does
not quite annul the earlier disparagement. Emerson does not
confront the possibility that the self may achieve a variety of
fulfillments, including some beyond the reach of Concord.
Why should he have supposed that the true self is to be cul-

---

*It is only fair to note that Emerson's reservation about Phillips was expressed
privately in his journals. Despite his critical feelings about Phillips' personality, Emerson did respond to the latter's call for public action against slavery.

tivated best or only in the woods or, failing that, in the study? That it must be private, insulated, unspotted? Is this a credo of human liberation or a mere local superstition?

Shortly after his praise of Phillips, Emerson records that he had received an invitation from him to speak at an antislavery meeting—an invitation that he, Emerson, esteemed "a command." And he went. One hundred and twenty-five years later we can still feel a glow of pleasure in knowing that he went. Yet it is hard not to wonder whether Emerson, even as he was now heeding his "moral sense," also realized that circumstance was slowly edging him away from the "project" he had seen as his life's work. For the "command" of Phillips, an outer voice of conscience, was blurring that side of him which John Jay Chapman so beautifully calls a "dry glint of the eternal."

III

THE LITERARY LEGACY

MEASURING THE INFLUENCE of "the newness" on American literature is difficult. These are not things to be weighed and counted, like items in a store. I venture cameo descriptions of three segments of American writing in the nineteenth century: the literature of work; the literature of anarchic bliss; and the literature of loss, announcing and mourning the end of "the newness." The literature of work is close in matter and spirit to the Emersonian vision; the literature of anarchic bliss winds its way around, sometimes against, the Emersonian vision, offering a paradisial glimpse that assumes the Emersonian vision, or any other republican idea, will be thwarted; and the literature of loss can be understood as a bitter reaction to the hopes of "the newness."

The literature of work, quite as fresh as the Emersonian celebration of "the plough, the shop, and the ledger," is fragile in substance and brief in span. Neither rising to the sublime nor deepening into tragedy, it is a literature that revels in the innocence of useful activity, glows with the freshness of unexhausted locale. It does not reject civilization, indeed, puts great store on a fine simplicity of manners; but neither does it tremble before the icons of the past, mourning over its belatedness. It avoids the harshness of a programmatic individualism, contenting itself with a modest independence. It draws upon the skills of craft. It falls easily into the comic mode, an open-throated musing on the slipperiness of life in a world not yet worn down.

Simon Suggs, rogue hero of "Old Southwest" humor, offers as his motto: "It is good to be shifty in a new country." Shifty can mean getting away from history as definition, moving easily through the spaciousness of a new world. Most nineteenth-century American writers like to be a little shifty, trying out a repertoire of selves as if the continent promised an endless supply, going out to sea in search of therapy and meditation, mastering trades without being mastered by them.

This American writing celebrates the satisfactions of craft, the wholeness of independent work. You can find these themes and attitudes in the early Melville and recurrently in Twain, and in some Whitman and Thoreau. For this benign mode of composition Emerson is the first caller. But what comes in counterspeech is not quite what he called for. The fictions honoring pleasurable work invite us to accept men as social beings; they do not worry about the "sublime presence" Emerson hoped to see as a luminosity of democratic man; or they assume that the face of an honest American mirrors as much of his soul as anyone needs to know.

Such writers as Twain and the early Melville want to picture the free-and-easy republican, sometimes a plebeian aristocrat like Captain Bixby or Jack Chase, who knows his work to the very essence of skill. Open, dignified, proud yet egalitarian, these men breathe a spirit of friendliness—but also reserve— toward other men and the natural world. This strand of American writing accepts the physical object and the social fact more readily than Emerson might have wanted, and it gets along very well in its casual self-sufficiency—it's the most good-natured writing in the world. Little of it survives the Civil War, and when Mark Twain writes *Old Times on the Mississippi* it is clearly with a backward glance, back to the time of "the newness."

Old Times on the Mississippi, one of the most beautiful of American books, opens with a lyrical celebration of work, a prose poem about the craft of Mississippi steamboatmen, and especially the river pilots supremely in command of their ships, their skills, their river, and, apparently in consequence, of themselves. "When I was a boy," reads one of the great openings of American prose, "there was but one permanent

ambition among my comrades in our villages on the west bank
of the Mississippi River. That was, to be a steamboatman."
The mild ripple of prepositional phrases in Twain's first sentence marks a new American style—we will encounter it later
in Hemingway; the narrative introduces a distinctive American figure, the independent craftsman who finds the meaning
of life in the substance of work—though by 1875, when *Old
Times* appears, this figure is starting to fade from the American
scene. In Twain's world he does not seek to go "beyond" his
work, in search of an elusive transcendence; he finds his true
self, neither outer nor inner, in his work, which requires, however, that he learn the face, the signals, the speech of nature.
All but impossible as it is to imagine a fruitful personal meeting between Twain and Emerson, a relationship of sorts does
emerge through their prose, testifying to the unpredictable
ways in which a culture may link apparently dissimilar figures.

In Twain's book the river pilots serve as an apotheosis of
human possibility. Feats of memory and concentration are
required for learning their craft: it is precisely the difficulty
that makes for the distinction. "My boy," says Mr. Bixby, the
master-pilot, "you must get a little memorandum book; and
every time I tell you a thing, put it down right away. There's
only one way to be a pilot, and that is to get the entire river by
heart."

Get the entire river by heart: is that not emblematic of the
high demands of craft? It means reaching a point where the
difference between work and play, work and art fades, and
what remains is the satisfaction of completeness. Twain's apprentice is both overawed and frightened as he submits to the
ordeal of training—there is a more traditionalist discipline
operating here than in Emerson or Thoreau, who might have
urged the apprentice to keep his own journal rather than
merely copy down what the master-pilot told him. But the
apprentice has his own green wisdom, rightly cherishing the

skill of Mr. Bixby. The apprentice takes pleasure in the pilots' shoptalk: how they boast of remembered feats, help one another through treacherous channels and passages. "Your true pilot," writes Twain, "cares for nothing about anything on earth but the river, and his pride in his occupation surpasses the pride of kings."

Once this boy has learned his craft, it seems as if the world will be ready to open itself to him. "The face of the water in time"—and here our apprentice gets about as close to the sublime as a busy working man needs to—"became a wonderful book—a book that was a dead language to the uneducated passenger, but which told its mind to me without reserve, delivering its most cherished secrets as clearly as if it uttered them with a voice." The man who has mastered his work can reach to the depths, the heart, the very essence of the world. I take this gratification to be social in character, Whitman's knit of identity perhaps. But it also depends on a natural piety toward rivers, trees, earth, and its pleasure draws on the thought that if you really know what you're doing, you may safely dispense with the Oversoul. Our satisfactions are to be found, the young Wordsworth wrote,

> in the very world, which is the world
> Of all of us—the place where in the end
> We find our happiness, or not at all!

A strand of the idyllic does of course pass through *Old Times on the Mississippi*. But the miracle of our native imagination is that the story should also seem so down-to-earth—or smooth-on-the-water—within American reach in the America that once was or could be summoned, quite apart from social transformation or personal transfiguration. A bracing air floats through Twain's book, an air of remembered strength and health. If there is anything of alienation here, it is the merest shadow of a shadow. *Old Times* indeed! We have never had another book quite like this, nor are we likely to.

The fulfillment of self through the sociality of work is only a secondary theme in *Moby-Dick,* set up partly in order to be torn down, and only occasionally granted the pleasing fullness it has in *Old Times on the Mississippi.* In his opening chapters Melville honors the fraternity of workers, men of all nations, colors, beliefs, who come together on the *Pequod.* In the sharing of the ship's tasks; in the strange, delicious ceremony of renewal that occurs when the men squeeze the spermatozoa of the whale; in the rough comradeship the sailors make for themselves: at all such moments it is work that enables Ishmael to escape from what Carlyle calls that "black spot in our sunshine . . . the Shadow of Ourselves." Wearied by that shadow, Ishmael goes to sea, and at sea one works. Queequeg, though a savage, also knows the civilized pleasures of work: he has "a particular affection for his own harpoon . . . like many inland reapers and mowers, who go into the farmer's meadows armed with their own scythes." But the plebeian brotherhood patched together in the opening chapters of *Moby-Dick* is doomed, perhaps by the onrush of history or, what may come to the same thing, by Melville's gloomy fascination with Ahab's overreaching. In American writing as it approaches our century, work as craft or independent venture will soon be replaced by heavy brutalizing labor which bends men to the machine's rationality, and only in a few writers will there be a backward look at that early republican America, the land of yeoman and craftsman.

In proposing to relate this thin but precious strand of American writing to the Emersonian moment, I have in mind something more consequential than influence. I have in mind "cultural fit," the way seemingly disparate or contrary elements of a culture can end in subterranean, even mysterious, connec-

tions. The nineteenth-century American writing I have out-
lined here forms a truly democratic literature, and to that
extent should satisfy Emerson's prescription; but insofar as it
rests mainly with a social or outer mode of existence and a
secular view of man's destiny, it cannot finally respond to
Emerson's call. For although he wanted buoyancy, health, and
good feeling, he wanted more. Only perhaps in Whitman
do the publicly democratic and personally sublime achieve
a fusion.

There is, by contrast, another and richer tradition of American
writing, one that, so far as I can see, has rather little relation to
Emerson. It proposes a vision of fraternal life where no man
can, or need, hold power over anyone else. This vision has
been described as pastoral, though for my purposes it is better
to speak of a native American anarchism, pacific and utopian,
locating its utopia in the past rather than the future. This line
of writing draws upon depths of the collective imagination so
profound that it might be described as "mythic," reflecting our
most hidden yearnings and secret griefs. Emerson in his essay
"The Poet" speaks warmly of the benefits of ecstasy and intuition—the intellectual, he writes, "is capable of a new energy
. . . by abandonment to the nature of things"; and myth might
be regarded as a culture's efforts to organize its ecstasies and
intuitions into enduring stories. Emerson himself, however,
was mostly a man of consciousness, not myth.

A paradisial dream haunts the imaginations of many American writers, and it hardly matters whether in explicit politics
they are Whig or Democrat, conservative or liberal: the dream
retains its power. It speaks for a state of nature not yet soiled
by history or commerce; it dares consider whether society is
good and, still more remarkable question, necessary; it summons a human community beyond the calculations of good

and evil, beyond the need for the state as agency of law and suppression, beyond the yardsticks of moral measurement—indeed, beyond all constraints of authority. A community of autonomous persons, each secure in his own being, grows out of the imagination's need. With it comes an assumption that because of our blessed locale we could find space—a little beyond the border, further past the shore—in which to return, backward and free, to a stateless fraternity, so that the very culture created on the premise of mankind's second chance would, in failing that chance, yet allow for a series of miniature recurrences.

It is in James Fenimore Cooper's *Leatherstocking Tales* that this vision first appears with the strength of detail, leaving its mark on American culture despite Cooper's dismal plotting and narcotic prose. Cooper's mind is that of a conservative democrat, but alongside or beneath mere opinion there flows a persuasion, a yearning for a state of social comeliness that he supposed to have existed among the Indians and located in his culture hero, Natty Bumppo. The conservative and anarchist impulses that jostle each other in Cooper's mind reach in Natty a union of serenity. Natty brings together the decorum of civilized life and the purity of natural man—precisely the unlikelihood of the mixture being what makes him so poignant a figure. Propertyless as a matter of principle and self-governing through ascetic training, Natty is a monk of the woods living in friendly closeness with Chingachgook, his Indian partner. Self and society here are at peace—at least whenever Natty is away from the settlements; or, better yet, in the moments when Cooper, so to say, gets out of Natty's way and society becomes absorbed into self, in a truce of composure.

Natty lives out the anarchist idyll of a life so beautifully attuned to its own inner needs and thereby so harmonious with the outer world that there is need for neither rules nor restraints. In the companionate space carved out by Natty and Chingachgook we have one of the few instances—imaginary, alas—where the Marxist prescription for the "withering away of the state" has been realized. With this proviso: that Natty keep moving steadily westward as state keeps encroaching upon forest.

The anarchist idyll of the conservative Cooper is one of the most influential elements of American literature. It is the name of Europe's desire, and, because the United States is the child of that desire, it is finally the name of ours too. And as in later fictional embodiments of this myth, the tone is finally one of sadness and defeat. At the end, in *The Prairie,* Natty may achieve a heavenly apotheosis, but he cannot stop the encroachments of the settlers and their corruption of the land. The paradise that almost was, the paradise that might have been, can only be mourned.

In a far greater book, Twain's *Huckleberry Finn,* where language and theme make an admirable fit and the only thing that cannot be resolved is the story itself, anarchic bliss resides, a fugitive, on a river. When Huck Finn and Nigger Jim are alone on that indispensable raft—so wonderful a symbol of the isolation, purity, and helplessness upon which the anarchist vision rests—they set up a communal order transcending in value the charms of their personal relationship. They create a community of equals, because a community going beyond the mere *idea* of equality.

The impulse behind the escape of Huck and Jim is toward a freedom that can neither be confined to, nor adequately described by, social terms. It comes into spontaneous being, not as a matter of status, obligation, or right, but as a shared capacity for sympathetic identification with the natural world, seen as a resource which can be tapped by those who revere it properly. It may be a sympathetic identification with other men, which is something to be learned, so that the learning becomes a way of moving past mere learning.

Huck's education is an education of the emotions. His decision to help Jim even if it means going to hell—a decision made without any conceptual grasp of the problem of slavery—becomes a triumph of nature over culture, anarchic fraternity over registered authority. In this state of friendliness men do not need society—at least so we learn in nineteenth-century American fiction.

When Huck and Jim achieve their moments of fraternal union, floating down the river, we are transported to a kind of ecstasy which enables them to rise above the fixed points of morality. Here the fragile note of the American sublime can be heard, not through the rendering of "shop, plough and ledger," but through a few pages marking the escapade of a boy and a slave, fugitive and helpless. As the raft takes them deeper and deeper into slave territory, Twain is making certain that we remember that paradise consists of a few rickety boards nailed together; that the raft contains a runaway slave worth eight hundred dollars; that violence threatens at every bend of the shore. Under the pressure of the world the anarchic enclave breaks apart. At one and the same time, Huck and Jim represent the power of transcendence, beyond the reach of society, and the pitiable vulnerability of social outcasts.

You can find variants of the theme of anarchic fraternity in the early Melville, more as recurrent temptation than fully developed narrative.* You can find the anarchic theme in Thoreau, as an enclave for solitaries, a nest for curmudgeons.

---

*How strong that temptation remained for Melville we can surmise from a poem he wrote in 1888, three years before his death, in which he remembers "Authentic Edens in a Pagan sea," where he had "breathed primeval balm / from Edens ere yet overrun," while now he wonders whether mortals can twice, "here and hereafter, touch a Paradise."

And oddly, even in Hawthorne, for whom freedom made its home in the woods, locale of erotic transgression and sexual happiness.

My distinction between the literature of work, all open air and open consciousness, and the literature of anarchic myth, all fantasy and yearning, is an analytic convenience. It simplifies, though we know that in actuality there is shading, overlapping, and complication. The literature of the independent craftsman survives, if at all, through a wistfulness of collective memory, while the writing that summons absolute freedom draws upon a mythic desire that seems to grow all the stronger as its plausibility becomes all the smaller.

The literary celebration of autonomous work has a basis in national experience; it may idealize what is past and gone, but it idealizes a discernible reality. The enchanting mirage of unconditioned freedom speaks for some deep compulsion in the American spirit, perhaps a regret over its own existence. As late as the final writings of Faulkner, this theme retains its force. In the beginning, Faulkner writes, was the wilderness, "almost pathless" and marked only by "the tracks of unalien shapes—bear and deer and panthers and bison and wolves and alligators and the myriad smaller beasts. And unalien men to name them too."

From the very beginning our most sensitive writers must have known in their hearts that things would not, could not, work out quite as the republican promise said; and so they lapsed, with a mixture of pleasure and sadness, into that mythic quest for bliss they knew to be a chimera. Once the figure of the independent American who works for himself and is beholden to no one was overtaken by history, then the Edenic myth would become all the more persistent, compensating for bewilderment and grief. Meanwhile, in the decades after the Civil War, still another voice comes to be heard in

American writing, the voice of loss and defeat, and here too, in a way, Emerson is its precursor.

When did "the newness" end? For that matter, when did English neoclassicism or romanticism? About beginnings, our literary historians are sometimes precise; endings are harder, perhaps less interesting, to locate. It is a common theme that the Civil War in all its bloodiness darkened the entire American landscape, bequeathing a social exhaustion in which idealistic impulses like "the newness" could only expire. I think this really began to happen somewhat earlier, during the 1850s, when the country shuddered with foreknowledge. In the 1850s a good many American writers lapse into a weariness that sometimes is called realism, as if to admit the futility of great expectations. About this time the pleasing identification of young America with the Roman Republic, symbol of austere virtue, becomes hard to maintain.

As early as 1841 Emerson is beginning to strike a note of uneasiness and self-doubt. Consider this passage from an essay written in that year:

> The genius of the day does not incline to a deed, but to a beholding. It is not that men do not wish to act; they pine to be employed, but are paralyzed by the uncertainty what they should do. The inadequacy of the work to the faculties, is the painful perception which keeps them still. This happens to the best. Then, talents bring their usual temptations, and the current literature and poetry with perverse ingenuity draw us away from life to solitude and meditation. This could well be borne, if it were great and involuntary; if the men were ravished by their thought . . . Society could then manage to release their shoulder from its wheel, and grant them for a time this privilege of sabbath. But they are not so. Thinking, which was a rage, is become an art.

Change a phrase or two and this might be taken for a lament written by an American intellectual of a later day, wavering between public engagement and a self-contained integrity. This Emerson, almost wistful in his self-doubt, seems one of us, and not at all the pumping, oracular author of "The American Scholar" or "Self-Reliance." But finally he is not the Emerson who matters most. The Emerson who matters most is the early Emerson: vatic, unmodulated, "promulging." Yet he too must suffer the course of disillusion that afflicts the culture once "the newness" has ceased to be new. In 1844 he published his great essay "Experience," uncovering to the public eye his inner wounds of doubt, while clinging as best he could to his earlier vision of a shared self-transformation. Perhaps a useful point at which to mark the exhaustion of "the newness" is that moment in 1851 when Emerson, raging against the Fugitive Slave Law, finds it intolerable that "this filthy enactment was made in the 19th century by people who could read and write. I will not obey it, by God." Once Emerson must yield to his social conscience, the newness fades. Voices of "the newness" will continue to be heard after 1851; two years later Emerson again attacks Wendell Phillips in his journals, discounting him as a mere creature of his movement; nevertheless, Emerson found that—like it or not, and a strong part of him did not—he was forced by conscience to become a little more active in the movement against slavery.

Had I been alive at the time, I would probably have been on Phillips' side, raising hell in fine Abolitionist style and scoffing at Emerson's fastidious refusal to join the good fight. It now seems to me that I would have been partly wrong, failing to recognize that if the urgencies of the moment were finally prodding Emerson toward the Abolitionists, that also meant he was being driven to abandon or compromise his true vocation. It was a vocation that committed reformers, then and now, could not always acknowledge. Insofar as Emerson was becoming a reformer pretty much like other reformers, his essential project, the glory of his younger years, had to dwindle.

Which is not to say that Emerson's partial involvement in public life brought no rewards. It did. There are strong new perceptions in his journals—never, alas, to be developed—like this one in 1846:

> Every reform is only a mask under cover of which a more terrible reform, which dares not yet name itself, advances. Slavery and Antislavery is the question of property and no property, rent and anti-rent; and Antislavery dare not yet say that every man must do his own work, or, at least, receive no interest for money. Yet that is at last the upshot.

So Wendell Phillips, toward whom Emerson was almost as ambivalent as toward himself, would be saying in the decades after the Civil War, at a time when his partner Garrison had retired and Abolitionism had faded into Miss Birdseye's memory. Barbara Packer, in her study of Emerson's inner development, has this cogent sentence: "The intellectual revolution of the early 1830s—the discovery of the God within—liberated Emerson from the hopelessness that had oppressed his [early or Unitarian] young manhood, but it could not do much for his stamina." It could not, first, because that "intellectual revolution" proposed no particular moment for realization, being truly a sort of Fabian prospect of permanent revolution, and, second, because it could not have anticipated the historical course of the country, especially the moral urgency which the struggle over slavery took on. Once Emerson was forced to think in time, and pay closer attention to his own times, his great moment came to an end. Anyone who has ever had to struggle with the conflict between public obligation and personal desire can only sympathize with his hesitations and uncertainties.

Emerson aged quickly. That often happens to writers who start brilliantly and then, in middle age, confront diminution. In "Experience" and "Fate" (1852) we see him twisting and turning: he is no longer the blessed Joseph of a free America; he is encoiled, like the rest of us, in circumstance, loss, depletion. Of the two essays "Experience" is the greater; "Fate" merely tugs the complexities of the earlier piece into the shallows of the explicit.

Sleep, he writes in "Experience," "lingers all our lifetimes about our eyes, as night hovers all day in the boughs of the fir-tree." The apostle of "the unfathomed might of man" discovers at the very root of his apostleship tokens of deadening, emptying-out. The seeker of rapture, who had announced himself a "transparent eyeball," now finds he is locked in "a prison of glass which [he] cannot see." The outer world is *there,* crushing, intractable, apart from our being, no mere shadow of self. All that speaks of inertia, sterility, dryness, the fright of inner limitation, takes over. And "we have no superfluity of spirit for new creation."

This is the language of inner life, used for a bleeding self-assault, self-excoriation. But there is also a hard look outward: we see the braves of the newness—"young men who owe us a new world, so readily and lavishly they promise, but they never acquit the debt; they die young and dodge the account; or if they live they lose themselves in the crowd." And with this, an impatient taunting of his earlier self: "I had fancied that the value of life lay in its inscrutable possibilities," but all is "an extreme thinness: O so thin!"

Voices intersect, in a dialogic torment; the skeptic assaults the believer, the older Emerson (forty-three!) harries the younger: "It is very unhappy, but too late to be helped, the discovery that we have made that we exist. That discovery is called the Fall of Man." Back against the wall, groping for some weapon, almost in rout: yet there remains "the Power which abides in no man and in no woman, but for the moment speaks from this one, and for another moment from that one." Earlier he had spoken of "a Persuasion that by and by will be irresistible," and the difference is notable, since a "Persuasion" suggests collaboration among men and women, while a "Power" would seem to come from elsewhere, perhaps the now-neglected Oversoul, perhaps the cold logic of evolution.

In the end, a dry season: "We live amid surfaces, and the true art of life is to skate well on them"—as if to mock his earlier depths ("I love all men who dive," Melville had said of Emerson). As for the culture on which he had put so many hopes, "with us . . . it ends in headache. Unspeakably sad and barren does life look to those who a few months ago were dazzled with the splendor of the promise of the times." Again, a return to the public theme. Emerson prods and pricks himself: "Life is a bubble and a skepticism, and a sleep within a sleep"—as if, fearful, he discovers in himself the spiritual tokens of a nihilism that lurks at the bottom of everything, not to be explored. Yet once more, as if to rouse himself: "thou, God's darling, heed thy private dream: thou wilt not be missed in the scorning and the skepticism." For "God's darling" that's not a very glorious justification for the calling of his life.

It is all astonishing, terrible, heartbreaking. Whoever has known the collapse of a large ideal will share Emerson's pain. How can anyone, encountering these bloodied pages, suppose that Emerson knew little or nothing of the evil, the losses, the tragedy, of existence? Still, he *is* "God's darling," even if forsaken, and he rallies himself at the very end: "Never mind the ridicule, never mind the defeat: up again, old heart!—it seems to say—there is victory yet for all justice; and the true romance which the world exists to realize will be the transformation of genius into practical power."

Emerson's critics are right, those who delicately respond to the inner curve of his thought and sensibility, his "train of moods," which soon enough, in his too-lengthy old age, will come to be "a sleep within a sleep." But I want to bring into play this other side of him: the Emerson who hoped to leave a burning mark on the life about him, the bearer of newness in or to the new world.

Hawthorne was not of course a devotee of "the newness"; he was its adversary. Yet some casting of fate or desire kept him in shadowy alignment with its history—as a sardonic double, a negative to its testimony. Several years after Emerson's "Experience," Hawthorne published *The Blithedale Romance* (1852), a novel brimming with mystifications which nevertheless suggest a kinship to Emerson's essay. Hawthorne was often prepared ironically to share in mourning for hopes he had not shared.

Sometimes prissy, sometimes passionate, *The Blithedale Romance* is an oblique exposure of thwarted desires and ideals associated with Hawthorne's Brook Farm experience, here rendered through techniques of displacement and mocking disguises. Melville was entirely right when he wrote that Hawthorne uses literary devices "directly calculated to deceive—egregiously deceive." Nothing in Hawthorne comes through openly, except those moments in which he abandons himself to sexual adoration of his dark ladies: Hester, his Puritan queen, and Zenobia, his Amazon queen. Just as anarchic pastoral liberates the imaginations of other American writers, so erotic violation followed by swift punishment serves Hawthorne.

"Whatever else I may repent of," says Coverdale, the spectator of passions who is the book's narrator, "let it be reckoned neither among my sins nor my follies that I once had force and faith enough to form generous hopes of the world's destiny." Punctuating the novel, such statements invariably are followed by biting disclaimers. When Coverdale leaves Blithedale, it is partly because he sees through the utopian impulse, discovering that ideal claims can shelter ideological fanaticism and personal inadequacy. "I was beginning to lose the sense of what kind of world it was, among innumerable schemes of what it might or ought to be." How odd that this should seemingly parallel Emerson's remark in "Experience": "It is very unhappy but too late to be helped, the discovery we have made that we exist. That discovery is called the Fall of Man"!

Hawthorne's tone is very different from that of Emerson or other apostles of "the newness." He lashes the utopian colonists for not managing to avoid the evil of the great world, but also, more shrewdly, for not entering a close enough relation with the evil of the great world. He beats down the male colonists; he kills off the opulent and threatening Zenobia; he destroys what had begun as a brilliant fiction by evading the lure of unsanctioned experience to which he had allowed himself to be drawn. And yet—just a little, feebly, ironically, like Emerson's self-encouragement at the end of "Experience"—he has his quavering Coverdale say about the utopian colony: "If the vision have been worth the having, it is certain never to be consummated other than by failure. And what of that? Its airiest fragments . . . will possess a value that lurks not in the most ponderous realities of any practicable scheme." The prophet and the skeptic, the essayist at the center and the novelist along the edge, each in his own way registers a breakdown of expectation, an end of the new.

How Melville felt about or responded to the Emersonian newness is a matter of some complication. I incline to the opinion of Perry Miller that Melville could not have reacted so fiercely against Emerson had he not earlier been drawn to him, less perhaps as thinker than as figure. Melville had his own newness. That is what made the 1830s and 1840s so exciting in America, that thinking persons could enlarge their minds, at once together and apart. Melville's newness was less a line of thought than a line of vision, across which strode splendid and bracing figures: firm democratic heroes like Jack Chase and Bulkington, in whom the conflict between fraternity and power was happily resolved. "Though bowing to naval discipline afloat; yet ashore, [Jack Chase] was a stickler for the rights of man, and the liberties of the world," even to the point of jumping ship in order to join a democratic revolution in Peru. For the early Melville the democratic ethos meant forging links with mariners, mutineers, and cannibals; filling one's lungs with the world's air; and receiving the blessings rightly due the elect of staunch republicans. The young Emerson and the young Melville were very different, but their differences serve finally to point up what they share as voices of the same moment.

Melville's ultimate darkness is more extreme, probably more profound than that of the aging Emerson. It occurs at a higher pitch of despair and is sustained over a longer stretch of neglect; it yields demonisms and nihilisms, grim refusals of all compensation, the force of which Emerson knew but which he often repressed beneath his glittering sentences. At the end both still want to "strike through the mask." Both are still stirred by the restlessness of an idealism reaching toward transcendence while bereft of a personal God.

Suppose Emerson had known the work of Melville's middle period; suppose he had read "Bartleby." How would he have coped with this bleak fiction, so apparently distant from his own way of taking the universe? I nervously venture a pastiche, aware that it is hopeless to try an imitation of Emerson's style yet hoping to grasp a little of what he might have felt upon encountering Melville's story. So here is a faked entry from Emerson's journal of the middle 1850s:

"A disturbing piece of writing comes to hand, a story by Herman Melville, once known for superficial sea stories. But this is not a superficial story, it is a depth fable. It bruises the nerves. It declares an undeclared war on my way of thought.

"Melville pictures a man, mild with the mildness of the deepest terrors, in a desolation almost complete. This author is not one of our milky American scribblers. He is a man who perceives the terror of life and has manned himself to face it. There is no compensation nor redemption. Bartleby is a soul emptied out, abandoned to its self; Bartleby is the rejected son of Fate.

"Herman Melville seems a man of our time, a metaphysician of doubt. But part of him still abides with our native ancestors, tormented by the fear of sin and thoughts of the Last Judgment. Worse than sin, which is active, is emptiness, which is stagnant. Emptiness is the greatest affliction we can know. In the life of this Bartleby—placed in Wall Street, but he could be in Concord also, down the road—Nature has become nothing, neither blessing nor presence. All we see is its negative, the tyrannous circumstances, the thick skull, the sheathed snake. Fate shows itself in shrinkage. A philosopher of fine shades, Melville knows that no picture of life can pretend to veracity that does not admit the odious facts, and nothing can be more odious than the way Bartleby is hooped by necessity.

"What order of mind could make a Bartleby? A mind that had once breathed the higher air of possibility. To reach this nothingness, a man must have passed through reflections upon everything. Melville must have been witness to our earlier, better days. His very denial keeps a spot of vision. Yet for me to say so may be too quick a comfort, for what is to be done with the Bartlebys of this world? Perhaps nothing, perhaps it is too late. I would resist both his maker and his meaning, though much truth is in both. Still, if Fate be all, a part of Fate is the freedom of man. Yes; but Bartleby? the haunting

Bartleby? He appears to be without will, that one most formidable weapon against circumstance. Is he then entirely supine?

"Not entirely. There is a thin margin of will. Pressed hard, Bartleby says: 'I would prefer not to.' And then not pressed hard, he says: 'I would prefer not to.' These are negatives that bleed with life. Drawing a line, Bartleby denotes himself. He makes a little space, and cannot a little space accommodate the infinite?"

Well, Melville never answered, except possibly in his caricatures of Emerson in *Pierre* and *The Confidence Man*. But surely he must have known these were not his last word; they were tokens of disappointed affection. In *Billy Budd*, his last word, he did essay an answer, not so much to Emerson or the world but to his earlier self. The exact purport of this answer we are never likely to know, so wrapped is it with ambiguities and maskings.

Billy Budd is a story so apparently inexorable in its logic and so attuned to the bitter rhythms of Fate that it comes to seem a myth, especially when we remember the bare story itself, apart from verbal setting. It is not a myth; it is a fiction written by a known author. But so hieratic and stripped does it seem, it takes on the necessity and mystery of myth. We grasp for parallels—Abraham's sacrifice of Isaac, Christ's preparation for the crucifixion—all stories of man's homelessness and transcendent suffering. At best these parallels are limited: Billy, innocent, stammers, while Christ, knowing, speaks. Billy is imaginable only as a creature of a yearning fixed upon utter comeliness of being, a yearning so absolute and intense, so powerful in its mirroring of desire yet so untenable in the life we must lead, that Melville's mature imagination apparently has no choice but fondly to destroy Billy.

In the story's bare outline—its purest variant, lapidary, mythlike—it posits a situation in which innocence must undo itself, victim to the world's malice, as represented in Claggart, a man of intelligence whose rage against Billy may stem from the anguish of unrequitable love but also draws upon a pure, unbearable envy before goodness acknowledged for what it is. Billy is victim to the world's "forms," as represented by Captain Vere, that decent and reflective man who, for all his dutiful virtues, acts out the impersonal justice—some would say, violence—of the state by justifying it in the name of a higher necessity. Vere and Claggart are fictional characters in the conventional sense, while Billy is a personification; which is one reason this story, though extremely moving, cannot be called a tragedy—there is no tragic hero. The story follows the tracks of necessity, and its conclusion, especially if torn out of its tonal context, is not so different from notions frequent in nineteenth-century writing: in Dostoevsky's *The Idiot,* whose marred innocent, Prince Myshkin, bears a cousinly resemblance to Melville's marred innocent, and even more in Tolstoy's diary for 1881 where we read: "The Christian doctrine cannot be lived. Then, is it nonsense? No, but it cannot be lived. Yes, but have you tried? No, but it cannot be lived."

That *Billy Budd* should have been embraced by conservative critics as "a statement of acceptance" or "recognition of necessity" is understandable. We all lie in wait for what we need. A version of this view appears in Lionel Trilling's novel *The Middle of the Journey,* where Maxim, the ex-Communist who transports the absolute from History to God, says of Melville's story:

> It is the tragedy of Spirit in the world of Necessity. And more, it is the tragedy of Law in the world of Necessity, the tragedy that Law faces whenever it confronts its child, Spirit. For Billy is nothing less than pure spirit, and Captain Vere nothing less than Law in the world of Necessity.

Before such weighty thoughts, straight or parodic, one wants meekly to murmur: I would prefer not to. Or at least ask: How necessary is this Necessity? Is it all ineluctably bound with the workings of a Necessity beyond our slightest shaping or does it result just a little from judgments of men, which, being those, are necessarily fallible and perhaps improvable? Must Captain Vere, in upholding the law, uphold it quite as he does? Is the necessity of punishment quite *this* punishment?

I believe that the chain of necessity in *Billy Budd* cracks at a crucial point. The sentence of the drumhead court, which Captain Vere upholds, is only an apparent necessity; there is a human decision being made here by not-at-all-godlike men which other men may doubt or dismiss. The trick of it all, a dazzling feat of technique, is that Melville creates a *surface* of necessity, suavely gliding past the crack that is actually there. For if the story is to convey the air of fatality we associate with myth and which Melville needs to set up as a barrier to his desires, then it must push everything to its limit. There must be a confrontation taken to its ultimate point, and this must end in Billy's defeat, so as to reassert the authority—or is it only the power?—of the powerful. Melville must deny himself the slightest possibility of slipping into what Nietzsche calls "metaphysical comfort"; this is a story of self-infliction. Yet comfort is just what conservative critics find in *Billy Budd*— comfort in declaring the need of submission to those social "forms," arthritic and unjust as they may be, which doom Billy but which they see as the foundation of civilized life. Even if these critics are right, there is something distasteful in the vindictive glee with which they proclaim their bad news.

Nor can much more be said for liberal critics who, detecting streaks of irony in *Billy Budd,* make it into a "testament of resistance," unwilling to recognize the distressing possibility that Melville had by now retracted the hopes of his early work, which in some sense also meant to withdraw from Emerson. That Melville's youthful truculence may still in small part be at work, that touches of irony may complicate and undercut his fable, seems plausible. Even more so, that the hermetic nature of the fable allows, not any reading, but a wide range of readings. Is it not likely, or at least arguable, that in dedicating *Billy Budd* to his old democratic hero, Jack Chase, Melville meant to signal an ironic contrast between wish and recognition, between resistance and submission? Or that in having Billy say "God Bless Captain Vere," just before being hanged, he was releasing a mordant irony with regard to the passivity of martyred goodness? Does Melville simply yield himself, without those reservations of thought and mood we find in all his work, to the definition of reality advanced by Captain Vere? If no longer a youthful rebel, does Melville still not reserve for himself a grimace about the way things are, even the way things must be?

We cannot be sure. Irony is not a fixed point, it is a moving field. It can modify many visions of the world, from Promethean defiance to broken resignation. The text, itself uncertain, gives us no fixed conclusion as to whether Melville intended only one response, or if he really knew which he intended. In "Bartleby" the character is up against the wall; in "Billy Budd," the author.

The accomplished editors of *Billy Budd,* Harrison Hayford and Merton Sealts, Jr., report that Melville kept changing the tonal ring of the story, mostly in behalf of a sharpening criticism of Vere. "The cumulative effect—whatever the intention—of [Melville's late] deletions and insertions . . . was to throw into doubt not only the rightness of Vere's decision . . . but also the narrator's own position concerning him." This pattern of perhaps obsessive changes exactly fits all that we know of the earlier Melville's inner struggles. He had created an extraordinary mythlike story, but what to make of it, which tonal signature to give it, how finally to judge it, he could not be certain. Who can?

Finally, Melville was trapped by his own imagining. He drove his story to its irreducible pain and outrage, as in the concluding three chapters where Billy is dead, but neither historical reports nor legends of the sea do his ordeal any justice whatsoever. If there *is* a last word here, it belongs to the Italian poet Eugenio Montale: "In *Billy Budd* the life which gives expression with equal violence to good and evil, right and wrong, tries, but without success, to solve its own mystery."

For American writers who spent their old age in the post–Civil War years, life grew harder—life in the ordinary sense of getting by and earning a living, also life in a sense special to writers of high aspiration now suffering fractured purpose, receding audience, and crumbling subjects. Melville stayed with private life, dignified, grim, silently productive. Whitman struggled in "Democratic Vistas" to apply an Emersonian vision to a society of mass production and mass culture, after which he settled into a cult for which he agreed to serve as idol. Emerson slid off into a benign acquiescence, kindly and a little sad, "a sleep within a sleep." The "newness" gradually became a subject for reminiscence and study, surest of signs that its energy was done.

But the Emersonian is the canniest of American vocabularies. As social creed it grew limp, a soft harmless idealism of nostalgia—except when turned to the uses of Social Darwinist reaction. For this, Emerson has to take some responsibility since, like Marx, he had not been very careful to protect himself against disciples. But the surprise of it all would be that, while declining in the America of the Gilded Age, and all the later gildings, into a manipulable sentiment, Emersonianism remained sharp, strong, and critical in our culture. It is everywhere among us, visible in writers who align themselves with its claims, but also, perhaps still more, in those who resist it, often after an earlier attachment.

"The newness" will come again. It is intrinsic to our life. It can take many forms, my own hope being for a difficult mixture of social liberalism and a reaffirmed and critical sense of self. But it will return, failing in success, succeeding in failure, "the green light, the orgiastic future."

Simple Emersonians we can no longer be. We are descendants, through mixed blood, who have left home after friendly quarrels. Yet the patriarch's voice still rings clear: "This confidence in the unsearched might of man belongs . . . to the American Scholar . . . Patience—patience . . . A nation of men will for the first time exist."

Patience? After all these bitter years? Darkened with the knowledge of loss, he speaks again: "Never mind the ridicule, never mind the defeat; up again, old heart!—it seems to say—there is victory yet for all justice."

NOTES

I. EMERSON AND HAWTHORNE

4 Bewley, "Puritan agnostic": *The Eccentric Design* (New York, 1959), p. 124.

4 RWE, "a mischievous notion": *Essays and Lectures* (New York, 1895), p. 65.

7 RWE, "men whom God": *The Journals and Miscellaneous Notebooks of Ralph Waldo Emerson,* ed. William Gilman, Alfred R. Ferguson et al. (Cambridge, Mass., 1960–1982), hereafter referred to as *J,* April 4, 1831.

7 RWE, "work a pitch": "Circles," *Emerson: Essays and Lectures* (New York, 1983), hereafter referred to as *E,* p. 406.

7 RWE, "glad to the brink of fear": "Nature," *E,* p. 10.

8 RWE, "our God of tradition": *J,* November 21, 1834.

8 RWE, "Within and Above": *J,* December 21, 1834.

8 Whitman, "for what they are worth": "Song of Myself," 41.

8 RWE, "You must be humble": *J,* October 1, 1832.

9 "one critic": Howard Mumford Jones, *Belief and Disbelief in American Literature* (Chicago, 1967), p. 66.

9 RWE, "rejection of all standards": "Self-Reliance," *E,* p. 274.

9 RWE, "law of consciousness": ibid.

9 RWE, "They call it Christianity": *J,* June 21, 1838.

10 RWE, "the Devil's child": "Self-Reliance," *E,* p. 262.

11 RWE, "There is never a beginning": "The American Scholar," *E,* p. 55.

11 RWE, "simplest person who . . . worships": "The Oversoul," *E,* p. 398.

12 RWE, "wear old shoes": *J,* April 1838.

13 Barth, "undercover apotheosis": Introductory Essay, Ludwig Feuerbach, *The Essence of Christianity* (New York, 1957), p. xxii.

13 RWE, "Alas, I know not": "Love," *E,* p. 328.

13 Arvin: "The House of Pain: Emerson and the Tragic Sense," *Hudson Review* (Spring 1959), pp. 37–53.

14 RWE, "laws of moral nature": "Nature," *E,* p. 24.

14 RWE, "nothing is got": "Power," *E,* p. 971.

14 RWE, "some levelling circumstance": "Compensation," *E,* p. 288.

14 Hawthorne, "After such wrong": *The House of the Seven Gables,* ch. XXI; italics mine.

16 Henry Adams, "Except for Negro slavery": *History of the United States of America During the First Administration of Thomas Jefferson* (New York, 1903), I, 159.

17 Jefferson, "insurrection . . . of science": Letter to John Adams, *Jefferson: Writings* (New York, 1984), p. 1309.

17 Jefferson, "Our revolution commenced": Letter to Major John Cartwright, ibid., p. 1490.

18 RWE, "stand on the ground": *J*, November 1863.

18 Paine, "a birthday": *Common Sense, The Living Thoughts of Tom Paine* (New York, 1940), p. 87.

18 Jefferson, "heavenly country": Letter to Elbridge Gerry, *Jefferson: Writings*, p. 1044.

18 Whitman, "My eyes settle": "Song of Myself," 10.

18 Jefferson, "chapter in the history": Letter to Dr. Joseph Priestley, *Jefferson: Writings*, p. 1086.

19 RWE, "and his great mates": *The Letters of Ralph Waldo Emerson*, ed. Ralph Rusk (New York, 1939), p. 298.

19 RWE, "What business": *J*, October 14, 1841; italics mine.

20 RWE, Things . . . saddle, "Things . . . snake": "Ode, Inscribed to W. H. Channing."

21 Whitman, "I find letters": "Song of Myself," 48.

21 Marx, "to recognize man's consciousness": quoted in Alfred Kazin, *An American Procession* (New York, 1984), p. 25.

21 Fredrickson, "to make way": *The Inner Civil War* (New York, 1965), pp. 7–8.

22 RWE, "All spiritual or real power": *J*, April 1848.

22 RWE, "The revolutions that impend": "Introductory Lecture," *The Complete Works of Ralph Waldo Emerson*, ed. Edward Waldo Emerson (Boston, 1903), I, 181.

22 RWE, "After all the deduction": "The Young American," *E*, p. 228.

23 O. W. Firkins, "hunger": *Ralph Waldo Emerson* (Boston, 1915), p. 169.

23 Whicher, "believer": Stephen E. Whicher, *Selections from Ralph Waldo Emerson* (Boston, 1957), p. xxi.

23 Robespierre, "We want": quoted in Philip Dawson, *The French Revolution* (Englewood, N.J., 1967), p. 131.

23 Trotsky, "It is difficult": *Literature and Revolution* (New York, 1957), p. 256.

24 David Ben Gurion, "The most important": quoted in Enzo Sereni and R. P. Asbery, *Jews and Arabs in Palestine* (New York, 1936), p. 125.

24 Adams, "Could America": *History of the United States of America*, I, 184.

25   Ortega y Gasset, "The cities": *The Revolt of the Masses* (New York, 1950), p. 7.

25   Chiaromonte, "Not finding room": "The Individual and the Mass," *Dissent* (Spring 1957), p. 168.

25   Valéry, "The inhabitant": quoted in Walter Benjamin, *Illuminations* (New York, 1969), p. 174.

26   Heilbroner, "is peopled": Robert L. Heilbroner, *The Nature and Logic of Capitalism* (New York, 1985), p. 131.

II. DISCIPLES AND CRITICS

29   Mailer, "a new kind": *Armies of the Night* (New York, 1968), p. 288.

29   Porter, "a first experience": "Conversations with Fairfield Porter," June 6, 1968, Archives of American Art, Whitney Museum brochure, 1984.

29   Scholem, "plastic hour": personal conversation.

30   RWE, "pervaded by nerves": "Pan," *Emerson's Complete Works,* Riverside ed. (Cambridge, Mass., 1896), IX, 309.

30   RWE, "argument burns": *The Complete Works of Ralph Waldo Emerson,* Centennial ed. (Cambridge, Mass., 1905), V, 337.

30   RWE, "Far off, no doubt": *J,* October 1835.

31   RWE, "among partial men": "The Poet," *E,* p. 448.

31   RWE, "to turn the world": "The Poet," *E,* p. 456.

32   RWE, "The Poet should install": *J,* June 27, 1846.

32   a washerwoman: quoted in Rebecca Richmond, *Chautauqua: An American Place* (New York, 1943), p. 24. (My thanks to Frederick J. Antczak for this reference.)

32   RWE, "My doom": quoted in Frederick J. Antczak, *Thought and Character: the Rhetoric of Democratic Education* (Ames, Iowa, 1985), p. 95.

33   RWE, "our poor little thing": *Correspondence of Carlyle and Emerson,* ed. Charles Eliot Norton (Boston, 1883); quoted in Gay Wilson Allen, *Waldo Emerson* (New York, 1981), p. 359.

33   Sarah Clarke: *J,* September 12, 1840.

34   RWE, "My dear Henry": *J,* May 11, 1858.

35   Thoreau, "a man more right": *Civil Disobedience.*

35n RWE, "Thoreau is like the woodgod": *J* (LM), 1848.

36   Thoreau, "Many are ready": "Life Without Principle," *The Writings of Henry David Thoreau* (Boston, 1906), IV, 463.

36   Thoreau, "The ways by which": ibid., p. 458.

36   Thoreau, "my connection with": ibid., p. 460.

37   Whitman, "Only the lull": "Song of Myself," 5.

39   RWE, "not good citizens": "The Transcendentalist," *E,* p. 202.

39   RWE, "Society also has": ibid., p. 208.

39   Hazlitt, "About the time": quoted in David Bromwich, *Hazlitt, the Mind of a Critic* (New York, 1983), p. 413.

40   RWE, "It is the part of a fanatic": *J*, July 1846.

40   Henry James, "field of consciousness": quoted in Alfred Kazin, *An American Procession* (New York, 1984), p. 174.

41   RWE, "in perfect eloquence": *J*, 1838.

42   RWE, "Heaven walks": Letter to Margaret Fuller, October 2, 1840(?), in *The Letters of Ralph Waldo Emerson*, ed. Ralph Rusk (New York, 1939), II, 352.

42   RWE, "as large as nature": Stephen E. Whicher, *Selections from Ralph Waldo Emerson* (Boston, 1957), p. 86.

42   Lukes, "Abstract Individual": *Individualism* (Oxford, Eng., 1973), p. 146.

43   Bradley, "the 'individual' apart": "My Station and Its Duties," *Ethical Studies* (Oxford, Eng., 1927), p. 173.

43   Marx, "Since the individual": Karl Marx, *Introduction to the Critique of Political Economy*, quoted in Lukes, *Individualism*, p. 76.

44   Berlin, "I wish my life": Isaiah Berlin, *Four Essays on Liberty* (Oxford, Eng., 1969), quoted in Lukes, *Individualism*, p. 55.

45   Rashi, "God came down": Rashi, *Commentaries on the Pentateuch* (New York, 1970), p. 44.

45   Silone, "pitiful, farcical sight": Ignazio Silone, *Emergency Exit* (New York, 1968), p. 1.

46   Mellow, "a conventional story": James Mellow, *Hawthorne* (Boston, 1980), p. 62.

51   RWE, "the masses": "Considerations by the Way," *E*, p. 1081.

52   RWE, "Nature by Trade": *J* (E), 1839.

52   RWE, "money . . . in its effects": "Nominalist and Realist," *E*, p. 578.

52   Freud, "special tendency to reduce": *The Interpretation of Dreams*, pt. I (London, 1953), p. 318.

53   Brownson, "would have all men": "The Laboring Classes," in George Hochfield, ed., *Selected Writings of the American Transcendentalists* (New York, 1966), pp. 258, 259–260.

54   RWE, "each 'cause' ": "The Transcendentalist," *E*, p. 203.

54   Pocock, "individual as civic": J. G. A. Pocock, *The Machiavellian Moment* (Princeton, N.J., 1975), p. 523.

54   Pocock, "dimension of historical pessimism": ibid., p. 541.

56   RWE, "I am in many respects": *Letters of Ralph Waldo Emerson*, ed. Ralph L. Rusk (New York, 1939), II, 369.

56   RWE, "I do not wish to remove": *J*, October 17, 1840.

57   Hawthorne, "as regarded society at large": Nathaniel Hawthorne, *The Blithedale Romance*, ch. III.

58   Hawthorne, "a young man had better": *The House of the Seven Gables,* ch. XII.

58   RWE, Brook Farm "of life-long value": *J,* August–September 1866.

59   Chapman, "The Greatest saints": John Jay Chapman, "The Life of Garrison," *Selected Writings of John Jay Chapman,* ed. Jacques Barzun (New York, 1957), p. 110.

59   RWE, "this filthy enactment": *J,* July–October 1851.

59   RWE, "I waked at night": *J,* August 1852.

60   RWE, "Very dangerous": *J,* 1853–1854?

60   RWE, "the supreme merit": *J,* February 1861.

61   Chapman, "dry glint of the eternal": Chapman, "Life of Garrison," p. 110.

III. THE LITERARY LEGACY

65   RWE, "the plough": "The American Scholar," *E,* p. 69.

65   Simon Suggs: quoted in Kenneth Lynn, *Mark Twain and Southwestern Humor* (Boston, 1959), p. 79.

68   Wordsworth, "in the very world": *The Prelude,* book XI, 142–144.

72   "anarchist idyll": I have adapted a few paragraphs from "Anarchy and Authority in American Literature" in Irving Howe, *Decline of the New* (New York, Harcourt Brace Jovanovich, 1970), pp. 99–106 passim.

73n Melville, "Authentic Edens": "To Ned," *The Collected Poems of Herman Melville,* ed. Howard P. Vincent (Chicago, 1947), p. 201.

74   Faulkner, "almost pathless": *Requiem for a Nun,* Act Two.

75   RWE, "genius of the day": "Introductory Lecture," *The Collected Works of Ralph Waldo Emerson,* ed. Robert E. Spiller and Alfred R. Ferguson (Cambridge, Mass., 1971), pp. 179–180.

77   RWE, "Every reform . . . a mask": *J,* May–June 1846.

77   Packer, "intellectual revolution": Barbara Packer, *Emerson's Fall* (New York, 1982), p. 154.

78   RWE, "It is very unhappy": "Experience," *E,* p. 487.

79   RWE, "We live amid surfaces": "Experience," *E,* p. 478.

79   Melville, "I love": Letter to Evert Duyckinck, 3 March 1849, in *Herman Melville: Representative Selections,* ed. Willard Thorp (New York, 1938), p. 372.

79   RWE, "Never mind the ridicule": "Experience," *E,* p. 492.

80   Melville, "calculated to deceive": "Hawthorne and His Mosses," in *Herman Melville, Representative Selections,* ed. Thorpe, p. 342.

80   Hawthorne, "Whatever else I may repent": *The Blithedale Romance,* ch. 2.

81   Hawthorne, "I was beginning": ibid., ch. 16.

81   Hawthorne, "If the vision": ibid., ch. 2.

81 Miller: "Melville and Transcendentalism," *Moby-Dick Centennial Essays* (Dallas, 1953).

85 Tolstoy, "The Christian doctrine": diary, May 29, 1881; quoted in Henri Troyat, *Tolstoy* (New York, 1965), pp. 426–427.

85 Trilling, "tragedy of Spirit": *The Middle of the Journey* (New York, 1947), p. 155.

87 Hayford and Sealts, "The cumulative effect": Harrison Hayford and Merton M. Sealts, Jr., eds., *Billy Budd, Sailor* (Chicago, 1962), Introduction, p. 34.

88 Montale, "In *Billy Budd*": Eugenio Montale, "An Introduction to *Billy Budd*," *Sewanee Review* (Summer 1960), pp. 419–422.

89 RWE, "This confidence in": "The American Scholar," *E*, p. 70.

INDEX OF NAMES AND TITLES